FINANCIAL FUTURES MARKETS

FINANCIAL FUTURES MARKETS

Brendan Brown   Charles R. Geisst

St. Martin's Press   New York

All rights reserved. For information, write:
St. Martin's Press, Inc., 175 Fifth Avenue, New York, NY 10010
Printed in Great Britain
Published in the United Kingdom by The Macmillan Press Ltd
First published in the United States of America in 1983

ISBN 0–312–28955–3

Library of Congress Cataloging in Publication Data

Brown, Brendan, 1951–
  Financial futures markets.

  Includes index.
    1. Interest rate futures.   2. Stock index futures.
3. Forward exchange.   4. Speculation.   I. Geisst,
Charles R.   II. Title.
HG6024.5.B76   1983   332.64'4   83–11001
ISBN 0–312–28955–3

For Irene Brown and Margaret Ann Geisst

Contents

List of Tables

List of Figures

Preface

Speculation, arbitrage, hedging, scalping and broking are the stuff of which futures markets are made. *Financial Futures Markets* presents a rigorous description of these five fundamental activities in interest-rate, currency, bond and stock futures markets. No attempt is made to simplify the operations of market participants for the purpose of presentation, as we believe that most readers would have the complete facts rather than an abridged version. Someone wanting to become a proficient chess or bridge player has to read conventions and rules in full, and it is no different in the futures markets.

Financial Futures Markets does more than provide an account of trading practices and conventions. It also presents an economics of the new markets. Issues under the economics heading include the measurement of currency and interest-rate risk exposure, with a clear distinction being drawn between economic and accounting risk; the relation of futures to cash prices and how this is determined by arbitrage transactions; the conditions of successful innovation, both of individual contracts and of market-places; and how the price and number of seats on the futures exchange are determined.

Chapter 1 is intended as an overall introduction to financial futures markets and should be easily readable by those who are starting from a low level of familiarity with the topic. Here the reader will find definitions and a simple introduction to what futures were originally designed to accomplish. The subsequent chapters deal in greater detail with individual sectors in the futures market. Currency futures are the subject of Chapter 2, where particular attention is focused on the relation of the futures to the forward market. Some new ideas are presented on how each investor should 'discover' the currency composition of his minimum-risk portfolio. Chapter 3 is concerned with money market futures. In addition to treating the five fundamental activities in futures markets, the chapter develops the concept of economic exposure to interest-rate risk and shows how this is intimately related to the investor's choice of horizon date. Chapter 4 describes the bond and Government National Mortgage Association futures and also provides a general description of the US Treasury bond market and the British gilt market. It also covers general yield curve considerations. Chapter 5 concludes with a general overview of what makes a futures market or individual futures contract successful, and also discusses how the price of seats is determined, how new exchanges are set up and who bears the risk, the uses of stock index futures, and interest-rate options.

Writing was divided between the authors by chapter content. Chapters 1 and 4, and the options section of Chapter 5, were written by Charles R. Geisst. Chapters 2 and 3, and the non-options section of Chapter 5, were written by Brendan Brown.

B.B.
C.R.G.

1 Concepts and Techniques

When asked how it felt to be approaching his eighty-fifth birthday, Clement Attlee once remarked that, all things considered, it was certainly better than the alternative. This comment succinctly embodies the uncertain conflict that the future psychologically imbues in anyone who must plan for it. And much has been made of the future in literature as well. During the late 1960s and 1970s, futuristic studies became fashionable in university curricula as social scientists delved into the problems caused by dwindling resources, over-industrialisation and war. But once the controversy, romance and mystique are stripped from the topic, one essential element about the future remains.

If one were to ask one hundred people about their definition of the future one could almost be sure of a hundred different responses (admittedly, a 'no opinion' could be somewhat worriesome in itself). Besides being inevitable, however, it would generally be agreed by most people that the uncertainty it suggests should be somehow hedged. But this naturally depends upon the stakes involved.

Hedging the future certainly does take some of the spice out of life but, in financial terms at least, it does help keep the proverbial wolf of economic loss from the door. In most financial markets it is considered *de rigeur* by most primary users of the commodity or instrument involved because of the potentially enormous economic consequences. The more volatile the sources of supply and demand, the more acute the need to mitigate risk. The one essential fact that emerges from all notions of the future is then simply this: future value is based primarily upon present value plus an element of time

1

risk. In this sense the future is not in another time dimension; it is only an extrapolation of the present.

In finance, as in any other field, planning for the future takes many forms. The decision-making process surrounding a capital investment project requires a projection of the estimated costs of the undertaking as well as the estimated benefits eventually derived. Also built into the calculations, especially during periods of high inflation, is an estimate of cost overruns given that the price of materials and labour may escalate over the life of the project. But regardless of the nature of the undertaking, the very nature of the process requires an estimate of present versus future value.

What exactly is implied in the comparison of present and future value? An optimist would probably argue that future value should normally be higher than present value in an investment sense with few exceptions. Otherwise the idea of progress and return on capital invested would be meaningless. However, the exception to this would be future value in an inflationary environment. In this case, the optimist would be more likely to hope for lower prices in the future so that the intrinsic value of his goods are maintained rather than eroded by further spiralling costs.

Although this is fairly commonsensical, it is also obvious that price is certainly not the sole determinant of assessing value although it is the primary factor in all financial markets. As will be seen many times in the following pages, price alone is complemented in the short- and long-term debt markets by the concept of yield, the true reflective indicator of value.

For many years, extrapolating the price of raw materials for future delivery has been common in the commodity futures markets. This was done in order to give anyone interested in using a commodity a benchmark upon which to base future expectations and calculations. The extrapolation itself is reflective of a multiplicity of factors, all of which centre upon expectation levels. If the price of a commodity is expected to be lower in six months' time than it is today, one must look to the various supply and demand factors which will, or can be anticipated to, affect it over that period so that its current futures price reflects all that can be reasonably known about the future. And as we shall also see, the future in this sense can have many graphical representations.

The reasons why commodities trade for future value are based upon purely practical considerations. A manufacturer cannot gamble on the cost of a commodity necessary to his business in the near term by simply keeping his fingers crossed and hoping it does not rise in cost. The process of adding value to goods requires that this type of uncertainty and the risks accompanying it be mitigated. Hence, the basic function of a futures market is integral to the value-added process; in order to create a future store of value, the interim costs of producing that value must be controlled.

Traditionally, commodity futures markets have been associated with agricultural and mining products such as soyabeans, wheat, zinc or gold. The commodities themselves are normally in raw material form; that is, they are not finished products although they can be derivative products of the basic commodity, such as soyabean oil. In either case, the actual commodity itself is referred to as a *physical* as opposed to futures.

More recently, commodity futures markets have expanded to include financial instruments. The historical background to this will be found in the next chapter. While it is not strictly correct to include financial futures in the same category as agricultural or metallic commodities, it is the mechanics of futures trading rather than the specific nature of the instruments themselves that has originally attracted these new instruments to be traded on commodity exchanges in preference to the debt markets, where their underlying securities trade.

FUTURES MARKETS TERMINOLOGY

Despite the obvious differences between traditional commodity futures and financial futures, the basic terminology of the futures markets applies to both. One familiar with basic financial market jargon should be at ease with futures terms. However, it should be noted at the outset that, while terms remain similar, the difference between the financial futures markets and the physical markets upon which they are based, referred to as the *cash* markets, is very subtle and intricate.

At the outset here, a distinction should be made between futures and *forward* markets; the latter being the traditional market for future foreign exchange trading. However, the distinction is more than simply verbal. Forward markets are used for dealing in foreign exchange alone while futures markets are more expansive, including short-, medium- and long-term debt instruments as well as currencies.

Another basic difference between them is locale. Forward markets are over-the-counter markets made by international banks trading foreign currencies both for themselves and their customers. Futures markets are individually organised exchanges trading in auction atmospheres similar to stock exchanges.

Perhaps more important is the matter of credit risk attached to dealing in one market versus the other. When an investor (normally in this case a bank or large corporation) carries out a forward transaction with a bank, he has completed a transaction to avoid risk but at the same time has incurred another risk, this time with the bank itself. This occurs because the bank has acted simultaneously as agent in completing the transaction and has probably also acted as principal in mitigating its own exposure to the same transaction. This will become clearer in Chapter 2. If, for whatever reason, the bank cannot supply the required currency on the delivery date, the risk becomes obvious. As in any over-the-counter market a risk is incurred in dealing with an agent or dealer as an individual rather than with an organised exchange.

In the exchange environment, this sort of risk is absorbed by a clearing house which acts to ensure that all trades done by agents of the exchange (brokers) will be acknowledged and carried out in full faith. The clearing house makes these assurances from a pool of money made available by its respective members. Functionally, futures exchanges help shift the burden of risk in forward transactions from single institutions to clearing houses, especially designed to absorb such risk. This is not to imply, however, that the clearing house is in itself a better credit risk than an individual institution but only underlines the difference in kind between the two risks.

As Chapter 2 will show, foreign exchange can therefore be traded in both sorts of forward market but the nature of that trading and the various arbitrage possibilities it presents are somewhat different. In any event, both markets are fundamentally different from stock or bond markets in that, by virtue of their structures, they do not actually trade securities but contracts on securities; contracts nevertheless binding. This form of activity is more properly known as *certificateless trading* in that it is not witnessed by an actual security but only by a binding book-keeping entry stating a particular futures position.

The absence of an actual certificate can be explained both in practical and economic terms. Practically, it would be cumbersome to issue a certificate every time a futures transaction took place because, by their very nature, futures markets invite heavy volume turnover. Economically, the reasons emphasise the value of futures contracts as assets.

Any commodity futures contract, regardless of the physical it represents, has worth for only a short period of time. For instance, if an individual decides in December to buy a commodity futures contract for eventual delivery in June, the contract only has value during that six-month period. Put another way, his asset is short-lived, subject to daily price fluctuations and, perhaps most importantly, cannot be fully considered an asset until it is finally paid for in full, on final payment date. So for the period which it is held it can only be considered a partially paid asset or hedging instrument. Later in this chapter we will explain the actual mechanics of a contract and the leverage it provides.

Therefore, certificate trading differs from all other forms of proper securities activity in that it terminates in a short mandatory period. This characteristic is also true of listed share options, which, while not futures instruments *per se,* nevertheless share many of the characteristics associated with futures.

In order to set out and define these terms as precisely and practically as possible, we will use an example of how one trades futures contracts. But before doing so, a brief mention of the sort of individual requiring hedging opportunities should be made clear in general terms.

Suppose that a manufacturer of a product needs to import a certain component from Ruritania and that this component will be delivered in four months' time. To complicate matters, delivery must be paid for in Ruritanian roubles, a currency easily bought and sold on the foreign exchange markets free of restriction (convertible) and one for which a forward rate may be determined.

If the manufacturer does not lock in a rate for the roubles he will add yet another risk to the process of bringing his product to market. However, if he knows the price at which he can purchase roubles in four months' time, enabling him to build this into his final cost, then the risk is mitigated.

The currency therefore can be purchased for future delivery at a price determined today. The contract entitles the buyer to a specific amount of roubles at a specific price, regardless of what the price may be on the actual delivery day. Adverse currency movements in the interim will not affect the purchase price.

This does not imply that there are not other risks surrounding this process since the futures markets are certainly not static. It is possible that during this four-month period the rouble may weaken on the foreign exchange markets and become even cheaper than it is today. This would lower the cost even further had not the manufacturer already purchased a futures contract. Any temptation he might have to ignore his contract by selling it in order to buy cheaper cash roubles would be offset by the fact that the market price of the contract has also slumped so that no advantage of any sort is gained.

Purchasing for future delivery is not the only strategy that can be accomplished on the futures markets. Alternatively, it is possible to sell roubles for future delivery if a holder decides that he must have, say, dollars in several months' time. Obviously the only difference between this and the strategy of the manufacturer is that the seller must have actual roubles to sell or anticipate owning them in due course.

In futures parlance, both types of investor are said to be *hedging* a position; that is, they are offsetting a real or anticipated need with a contrary position in order to lock in a price. Now there are other types of investors who enter the picture here who have no real or anticipated desire to hold either dollars or roubles. These are the speculators who help provide the necessary liquidity which any market needs to function properly. But before we can elaborate on the value of speculation for the markets we must return to some basic terms.

The essential difference between a physical and futures market is that, in the latter, there is no actual selling of a security so all sales automatically become *short sales,* or shorts. In securities markets, short selling means selling a share or bond one does not own in order to purchase (cover) it at a lower price at a later date. In certificateless markets, all sales become *ipso facto* short sales. Anyone who hedges an actual long physical position by selling is said to be selling short. Conversely, someone who purchases for the future is said to be 'going long'.

Regardless of the position one assumes, the most funda-mental distinction made in the markets is the difference in *delivery months* of the contracts themselves. For instance, assume that the following quotations are found in a news-paper. The various months listed with a price are the months for which actual delivery can be effected. In Tables 1.1 and 1.2 June is referred to as the 'spot' month, in that it is the nearest delivery month and as such most closely approxi-mates the present value of the underlying physical commodity involved, in this case Treasury bills.

According to this example, the price of the bill for June delivery is 89 while that for September delivery is 89.25. Price quotations such as this are a virtual Pandora's box in that they contain much more information than may immediately be apparent.

Unlike securities, the size of a futures transaction is regulated. For example, one cannot choose the amount of Treasury bills to buy or sell without referring to minimum contract size. Since the bill contract is $1 million the investor must then trade contracts in multiples of that amount. A contract cannot be split into odd lots. And since financial futures represent money, bond and foreign currency market

TABLE 1.1   Treasury Bill Futures Prices*

June	89.00
Sept.	89.25
Dec.	89.30
March	89.40
June	89.50

* per cent

TABLE 1.2   Treasury Bond Futures Prices*

June	67.00
Sept.	67.08
Dec.	67.16
March	67.22
June	67.30

* per cent and 32s of 1%

instruments, in themselves normally traded in large amounts, the futures contracts tend to represent the average multiple in which these instruments trade. These three particular markets tend to be dominated by institutional rather than retail investors so the average trading lot tends to be large in the eyes of the individual.

Another fundamental of all futures markets is particularly important to financial futures – the *deliverable grade* of the case instrument involved. If a producer of food products buys soyabeans for future delivery he must be certain that those delivered are of the proper quality for his product. In the same manner, a buyer of long-term Treasury bonds needs to know that the bonds delivered will be liquid instruments, trading actively and interest-rate sensitive. The quality grade of all commodities is set out by the appropriate clearing house involved. This ensures some degree of consistency for those who use the markets for actual long or short hedges.

Why, it may be asked, should one want to purchase any financial instrument other than foreign exchange contracts for future delivery? Unlike metallic or agricultural products, they are not necessarily a part of manufacturing or productive processes. And as we shall see in the next chapter, the financial futures exchanges themselves are less than ten years old. Obviously, for over a century, American and British investors have been able to survive without committing themselves to future interest rate contracts.

The answer to this problematical question lies partly in recent monetary history and partly in the ever changing phenomenon of financial intermediation. Recent developments in the term structure of interest rates both in the USA and Britain, caused by several rounds of OPEC price increases and two subsequent recessions, have created a new dimension of interest-rate volatility and uncertainty in money and bond markets. The yield curves of interest rates in both countries, at one time accustomed to a sedate contour, began to gyrate quite wildly between positive and negative slopes.

This very volatility has caused many changes in the behaviour of financial intermediaries. Traditionally, institutional fixed income investment sought to give a specified yield over time, normally conservative in expectations, while at the same time protecting against capital loss. With the advent of volatile rates, many institutions, as well as individuals, saw the capital value of their holdings quickly erode. As it became apparent that this volatility was more than short-lived, the value of hedging fixed income portfolio holdings became obvious.

Financial intermediaries themselves also played a role in the disquietude suffered by the debt markets. Before financial futures became widely used, especially in the USA, incorrect assumptions by professional money managers about the future course of interest rates could cause severe strain both to the markets as well as the end investor whose money was being directly or indirectly managed. At present, about 75% of all money invested in both the USA and Britain is handled by professional managers. Incorrect assumptions on their part can cause severe strains on the financial system as a whole. A pension fund that is too slow to react to rate changes hurts its ultimate payee, the individual retiree, as well as the financial system upon which its subsequent actions can cause a great drag.

While financial futures do not have much direct effect or influence upon the traditional manufacturing processes, it can be quickly seen that their uses are equally as important in mitigating risk as are the more traditional types of contracts. But it should not be automatically assumed that futures help to offset risk totally; the best that any contract can do is to offset the larger part of any risks involved.

The most essential concept in financial futures trading is what is known as *basis risk*. This is the fundamental risk intrinsic to the trading process and is reflective of the two elementary topics already mentioned – deliverable grade and spot versus forward pricing. Without an understanding of basis risk one cannot presume to understand futures operations since it underlines the most simple maxim in the markets; there is no such thing as the 'perfect hedge'.

Imagine an investor who has a position that has to be hedged for six months by shorting a futures contract against it. Is any additional risk incurred by doing so? The answer is 'no' but it should be clear that one cannot perfectly hedge the position as such. But it should be noted that the process of hedging, while appearing to mitigate risks, possesses intrinsic pitfalls of its own.

In our example, the chance of the hedger actually hedging the holdings at exactly the same price that was paid for them is, in most cases, quite remote. And the deliverable grade may not precisely match the quality of the long position. In bond market terms, this can be seen quite clearly. Suppose that the investor held a 13% bond of medium quality and hedged it by selling a high-quality Government bond contract yielding only 12%. The difference in the quality of the two instruments is reflected in their respective yields. The 1% differential is known as basis risk; the difference in deliverable grade which cannot be hedged because of the discrepancy between the two instruments.

Basis risk can also be seen when attempting to match two instruments which differ in time, or term. This problem has two aspects. First, the hedger may find that the nearest delivery month to his own intended delivery date varies by one month. The price that he would hedge at will reflect the difference. Thus, he can only be certain of a hedge at that level where the two prices overlap. This type of time risk is quite normal in the futures markets because many delivery months will, as a matter of common sense, not match every individual hedger's wishes.

Secondly, and more intricately, time risk occurs when the long and short positions vary fundamentally in length to maturity. This is a problem unique to financial futures because only debt instruments have stated expiration dates. Unlike soyabeans or pork bellies, they are not normally subject to spoilage and only mature when intended. And it is in the multitude of maturity lengths in the money and bond markets that risk again becomes apparent when faced with more uniform futures contracts.

Basis risk is derived from the method by which yield is stated in the debt markets, that is, in *basis points*. One basis point equals 1/100 of 1%, or 0.01. Thus, the difference between 12% and 13% is 100 basis points. Basis risk is not only a financial futures term but no other commodities *per se* are stated in yield terms. The basis in the financial futures markets refers to basis points and all that is reflected in them.

In the following pages we shall discuss the three major types of financial futures – foreign exchange or currency futures, and money and bond market instruments. Each is measured in value by its relationship to the overall term structure of interest rates. This is perhaps most obvious for money and bond market instruments, themselves expressions of interest rates, than for foreign currencies. But before exploring these differences in Chapters 2, 3 and 4, the other basic concepts common to all of them need to be outlined since they are methods of succinctly summarising investor expectations.

There are many ways of describing investor expectations. Perhaps the most general market related term is also the most cumbersome to understand but through its very cumbersomeness it forces one to adopt a broader perspective when viewing futures prices than many market participants do. An optimistic view of the future is referred to as a *contango* while a negative view is called a *backwardation*. The former is an arrangement whereby an investor leverages himself (borrows money) in order to purchase securities and carries this position forward until he is able to sell at a profit. In general terms, future prices are expected to be higher than today's.

Backwardation refers to a situation where futures prices are expected to be lower than they are today. Put another way, plotting a backwardation would illustrate a negative slope in price.

It should not be assumed that contangos are always positive and backwardations negative. This is where the matter of perspective enters. In a period of high inflation futures prices also pointing higher suggests a continution of high inflation in investors' minds. In this case, a state of backwardation would probably be a welcome sign.

Both of these conditions are easily apparent in many markets where price is the only factor one needs to gauge the future. But since price is reflected in yield (and vice versa) in the debt markets, one must always remember the basic axiom of interest bearing securities: prices and yields move inversely from each other.

A practical example of this can be seen by examining the Treasury bill prices set out in Table 1.1. By plotting prices diagrammatically, it can be seen that these bill prices slope upwards, indicating a positive *price* curve for the future. But what of the yields? They, conversely, move down in the future.[1] This can be seen in Figure 1.1.

This suggests that Treasury bill yields are in a state of backwardation, being lower in the future than they are today. Whether this is good or bad ultimately depends upon the shape of the entire yield curve, not just Treasury bill rates alone. If the yield curve generally is negative, with short-term rates being higher than the long term, then this would be considered a positive factor in ultimately bringing about a positive yield curve again; where short-term rates are lower than the long term.

There are several caveats which should be kept in mind when examining futures prices. As a matter of discipline, one always begins with the *spot* month, that is, the price for the nearest delivery month. Proceeding from there, one must also note the amount of contracts existing for any given month. This is called *open interest* and can quickly illustrate whether or not there is enough outstanding volume on the contract

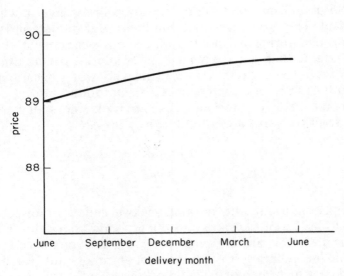

FIGURE 1.1   Treasury Bill Price Curve

vis-à-vis other contracts to suggest that its price/yield relationship adequately reflects investor expectations. At times,
certain future delivery dates may not have adequate volume
for technical or seasonal reasons and on that basis may not be
good indicators.

Added to these generalisations is another more specific
remark about futures prices made by both J. M. Keynes and
John Hicks.[2] In a state of equilibrium, where supply and
demand balance, futures prices for any commodity should
normally be in a state of mild or 'normal' backwardation. The
reason for this is twofold; first, if expectations are neither
overly optimistic nor pessimistic then the future price would
be the same as the spot but would not necessarily engender
much investor interest. As a result the price would slip to a
small discount from the spot level.

Secondly, and more specifically, for the instruments
described here, if this situation prevails the difference between the spot and future price should reflect the cost of
money for the intervening period. Imagine for a moment that
you are going on holiday in a month's time and decide to
purchase sterling with your dollars. The rate today is

$1.85/pound and you feel this is an appropriate level at which to deal. The problem is that you have your money on time deposit, maturing in a month's time and you cannot withdraw it. Assume that you are receiving 1% interest per month. If conditions remain as they are you need not worry because the month's future price will be at a discount to the spot.

In this state of 'normal backwardation' the spot versus future or forward rates would be as follows:

$/£ spot	1 month	2 months
$1.85	1.8315	1.8132

In equilibrium, the normal backwardation or discount, would be 1% of the spot, or $.0085/pound. Since this is the same rate you are currently receiving on your account it would be pointless to withdraw your funds and purchase sterling which may only lay idle for a month until you use it when you can leave them on deposit and actually purchase the currency marginally cheaper one month hence. Simply, the cost of purchasing at present can be matched, and in this case exceeded, by understanding future pricing.

Unfortunately, not all futures prices are as uncomplicated as this example. Nevertheless, it is true that all futures or forward pricing is based upon expectation levels plus the cost of money for the period involved. The more complicated aspect of this somewhat oversimplified description is aberrations in prices which give rise to subsequent arbitrage possibilities.

DEVELOPMENT OF THE MARKET

Commodity futures markets originally developed alongside the physical commodities markets upon which they were based. Although both types of trading have existed in one form or another for centuries, little is known about their precise historical development. However, it is known that commodity markets were the immediate predecessors of stock markets. The change took place in Britain in the seventeenth century when novel 'commodities' such as trade bills and shares in public companies took their place next to agricultural and metallic goods.

The contemporary financial futures markets developed in much the same way. Treasury bill futures made their début on the Chicago Board of Trade (CBT) in 1976. Until that time, the CBT was known primarily as a commodity futures market, not one specialising in interest rate futures. While it would have appeared logical that financial futures would have cropped up on a stock exchange or bond market, it was the trading mechanics of the commodity futures markets that proved more applicable than the capital markets. While a twenty-year bond and a soyabean would appear to have little in common, it was nevertheless convenient to treat them similarly for trading purposes.

Trading mechanics aside, when the initial bill contract was introduced, it had more curiosity value than practical interest. There was, at the time, no immediate need to hedge fixed income instruments, especially since American interest rates had just settled down again after the initial shock caused by the first OPEC oil price rise. When the twenty-year bond contract was itself inaugurated in 1977, medium and long-term rates had stabilised at levels below 10% and the idea of hedging at those levels, given the relative calm surrounding the yield curve, would have been supererogatory. During the first year of the bond contract's life, total volume of all financial futures contracts stood at less than a half million contracts traded. How these figures compare with subsequent years can be seen in Figure 1.2.

Domestic and international economic conditions dictate the need for hedging instruments and this is succinctly illustrated by the peregrinations of long bond yields after 1977 in the USA (Figure 1.3). As conditions became more and more volatile, an immediate increase can be seen in the level of activity in the representative futures instrument.

We have already mentioned the necessity of hedging fixed income assets in a general sense but to emphasise the point more dramatically it can also be viewed in money terms. In 1982, the estimated nominal capitalisation of the US Treasury note and bond markets was approximately \$752 billion.

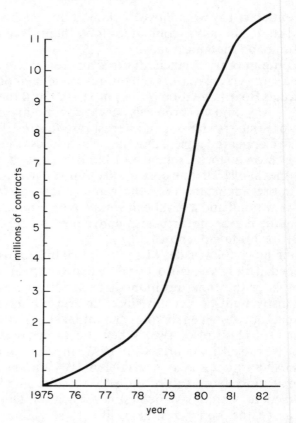

FIGURE 1.2   Growth of Financial Futures Contracts, 1975–81

During that year, prices rose and fell sharply, prompted by tight Federal Reserve monetary policy and a serious recession, following two years of erratic economic performance and high inflation. Also, when short-term interest rates pulled up the longer term and equally eroded investor confidence, many corporations were forced to borrow short at high levels of interest because long-term costs, without some sort of call protection to protect the borrower, were unrealistic. Following these events, a 1% drop in bond and note prices would represent a paper loss to investors of some $7.52 billion (calculated off nominal value). In reality, periodic losses could amount to several per cent at any particular moment.

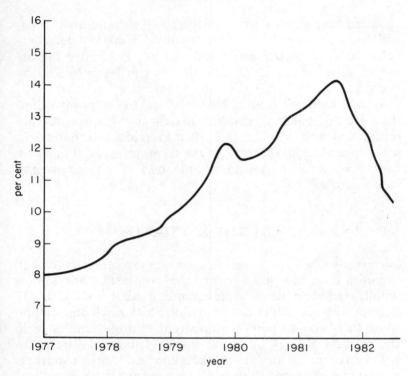

FIGURE 1.3   Long US Treasury Bond Yields, 1977–82

These sort of staggering numbers underline the importance of futures as means of mitigating risk.

In the United Kingdom, interest-rate conditions were slightly less volatile during the same period but the need for hedging was no less acute. The British financial futures market officially began with the London International Financial Futures Exchange (LIFFE) in 1982. Until that time, hedging sterling instruments was difficult at best. Naturally, the forward market existed for sterling foreign exchange dealing but hedging UK government stocks (gilts) was not a simple matter. Not all dealers could even execute a short sale of a gilt as a speculative gesture. In order to do so, the institution had to be assigned a 'Z' account by the Bank of England and these were not easily obtainable.

Despite what has been said thus far, it should not be readily assumed that anyone who holds a fixed income instrument will desire to hedge it. The costs involved, while not considerable, do nevertheless enter the picture. But more importantly, as will be evident, not all risk can be mitigated by hedging.

Today, financial futures have evolved to the point where they are no longer considered as just another commodity future and now warrant their own individual exchanges in some locales. And on some of the more traditional markets they have come to represent one half of all commodity volume traded.

ORGANISATION OF THE EXCHANGES

As already discussed, futures exchanges are centrally located organisations; the instruments they represent are almost wholly traded on the over-the-counter market in the USA. In Britain, gilts are dealt on the London Stock Exchange. While these facts may be painfully apparent to those familiar with the markets, it helps underline several structural differences between currency forward markets and bond and bill markets on the one hand and their newer counterparts on the other.

The reasons futures must trade on an exchange are twofold. Due to the fact that futures trading is fast and frenetic, a central location is necessary in order to execute trading in an orderly fashion. Actual price execution could not be achieved by telephone, owing to the nature of the auction process, which we shall examine below. But perhaps more importantly, all futures exchange trades are backed by a clearing house which has the responsibility of ensuring that orders are carried out and deliveries made, where applicable. The assumption of risk by a clearing house would not be possible in the over-the-counter market since there would be no centralised method of recording transactions.

The location of futures markets in the USA has functionally proved to follow traditional rather than wholly practical lines. The most successful financial futures market remains the CBT although attempts to institute competing markets have been tried in other money centres, notably New York.

An old, time-proven maxim of commodity futures markets has again been proved valid in the case of financial futures: the market must have local support. This means that the market must draw its liquidity from the presence of local speculators if it is to succeed. Although there may be no end to the number of real or potential hedgers in a market, without speculative counterparties, no deals can in fact be done. And speculators traditionally only supply liquidity in a market where executions and price movements are fast and potentially profitable, meaning that for the most part they prefer established markets. This circular sort of logic then also attracts the hedgers. In the end, experience has proved, at least in the USA, that the well-established commodity futures markets have remained in the vanguard of financial futures dealings.

TRADING MECHANICS

The actual market environment on the exchanges is organised on an auction basis; that is, price executions on a moment to moment basis are done at the best price available. The floors of the exchanges are structured on a pit basis. Brokers gather in a pit environment and communicate execution prices among themselves. There is no one particular auctioneer or specialist heading the process; it is conducted on a group basis. Brokers, or floor brokers to be precise, make their wishes known to this group *à crie,* or by open outcry. In fact, executions are done through a combination of outcry and hand signal, the latter signifying a positive response to a particular price.

Floor brokers, normally representing firms, are also complemented by floor traders who trade only for their own accounts. These traders, or scalpers as they are sometimes known, trade from minute-to-minute, sometimes contenting themselves with very small price movements.

The method of bid-ask quotations used in the securities markets is also used in the auction process on the respective futures exchanges. Those most familiar with capital markets will recognise the traditional spread used by floor traders;

that is, the price at which you sell (bid) versus the price at which you buy (ask or offer). The difference between them is the profit made by the dealer. Generally speaking, the size of the spread indicates the level of risk perceived by the dealer. Normally the smaller the spread the less risky the market in terms of liquidity overall and the supply of the security in question.

On the financial futures exchanges, the bid-ask spreads are similar to the spreads used on the underlying instruments in the cash markets. If a price of 90 – 90 1/4 is made in the Treasury bond market it means you buy at 90 1/4 (% of par) and sell at 90. A futures trader in bond contracts may use a similar spread although it will not necessarily be exactly the same price used in the cash markets. Additionally, the futures commission broker will pass along a commission to his client as well; in the cash bond and bill markets no commissions are charged. The spreads suffice.

The spreads mean similar things in futures *vis-à-vis* the cash markets. In the latter, a spread helps compensate the dealer for those securities which go unsold and need to be financed until a buyer is ultimately found. In futures, a dealer may actually build positions in the market in contracts which will ultimately require financing, and therefore positioning is a major function of futures traders as well as it is of securities dealers.

The auction floor of the futures exchanges provides a dynamic environment where constant liquidity is maintained in a two-way process between hedger and speculator. The most liquidity is normally provided in those delivery months near at hand, or close to the spot. But equally important to this entire process are the actual costs involved.

Since hedgers and speculators do not trade actual securities they are not required to deposit the full cash value of the nominal futures contract. They simply deposit a small percentage of the nominal value, called *margin*, which must be maintained throughout the contract's life. This margin requirement varies from contract to contract but normally amounts to about 2% of principal value.

This margin as such must be maintained and this is when the practical risk of trading enters the picture. If a contract's value moves against the investor, the amount of margin will erode along with the principal amount and must be topped up. Thus, in addition to the ultimate risk of being subject to price movements based upon the principal amount of the contract, the investor may also be subject to margin calls at any time.

Given the intrinsic price volatility on most futures exchanges, price *limits* are set on contracts. These limits are set both to protect the investor and maintain order on the exchanges. Their purpose is to protect against runaway price movements. But they do not imply that trading ceases once a limit has been reached. Imagine a bond futures contract which spurts two full percentage points in price; 'up the limit' in market parlance. No one may trade that contract again outside that price level. Any subsequent trading must take place inside the limit.

While limits give futures prices a breath of market stability they are not panaceas for volatile markets. It is possible for a contract to have a limit movement for more than one day consecutively. If this is the case, the contract can have moved several full per cent of its value.

A PRACTICAL EXAMPLE

With all of these concepts and mechanics in mind, we shall recapitulate this entire process thus far by giving an example of how one opens a hedge position. In this particular case, the simplest example will be used since more difficult strategies will be mentioned in later chapters.

Imagine that you are an investor, probably a fund manager or corporate treasurer, whose cash flows indicate that you will have $10 million to invest in six months' time. This cash, when realised and invested, should be kept in short-term money market instruments. Although this may seem an inappropriate moment to worry about the future, today's current rates are appealing and you would like to lock them in if possible. So you look to the futures market to see what is available.

The most popular short-term financial future is the US

Treasury bill. Bills themselves are the largest of all short-term financial instruments, regardless of currency of denomination. They range in maturity from about a week to one year. Assuming you were to buy bills today, imagine you would receive an annual return of 14%, or 7% for six months. Since bills are sold and traded on a discount basis (in both the USA and Britain), the yield to you is reflected in the discount price. This 14% bill, discounted for one year, would cost you 86% of the nominal value invested. For six months it would cost 93%.

If you decide that you would like to lock in this bill yield for six months in three months' time, you must not assume that the three-month future price will be the same as the current price for reasons already mentioned. The up-to-the-minute price can be supplied by your commission broker.

When you decide to buy for future delivery at the level the broker has reported, you may enter different types of buy orders. Basically, you may buy at the market rate prevalent at the moment or enter a limit-order, to purchase at a specific price or better (i.e. lower). Since you are buying $10 million of bills, represented by ten contracts, you may decide to enter a 'fill or kill' order within a certain range, meaning that your order must either be filled as stipulated or discarded.

At the same time, you must also be aware of the margin deposit requirement so that you know exactly how much money to place with the broker. As you do so, you also understand that the ultimate risk in this entire process from start to finish is with the particular clearing corporation backing the whole transaction.

As time progresses, you must keep track of the contracts' performance because you are at risk for the full principal value of the contracts, not just the amount you deposited. Interest rate movements in the interim can greatly affect the contracts' value. If rates rise above the 14% level the value of the contracts will fall and you could be subject to a margin call in order to maintain the value of your position. Conversely, if rates fall below 14% the value of the contracts will increase, presenting you with a paper profit. The important feature to remember here is that futures markets are not static arenas and hedging prices should be carefully monitored.

In this example, we are simplifying this process by using a

hypothetical long hedge. If the example were a short hedge, it would be incumbent upon the investor to determine at the outset his basis risk; again the difference in price, yield and maturity terms between the future and his actual long holding.

The execution of the order on the floor of the appropriate exchange is normally relatively easy to execute unless the market trades up or down the limit. Suppose that the Federal Reserve announces measures which are interpreted as bearish for interest rates and the bill price falls dramatically. If this occurs almost simultaneously with your order being executed on the floor, one of two general problems could arise: you could either be filled at the higher level before a lower price was realised, or you could miss the order entirely for the time being.

As time wears on and delivery date for the contracts comes closer you must now decide what to do with your position; in other words, how to unwind it. Assume that rates have indeed fallen during the interval and the contracts have increased in value. The question you are faced with can be simply put but may be more difficult to resolve: do you take the contracts' profit and re-invest the proceeds at the lower prevalent bill rate or require delivery of the bill called for by contract?

In either case, the net effect should be about the same. The majority of long hedgers close out the positions and presumably invest the profit in the new rate; the extra amount of profit enhancing the return on the lower yielding bills. The CBT estimates that only 1% of contracts actually call for a delivery. Would you violate your original strategy by cashing in rather than proceeding to the last stage?

In order to keep the example simple, assume that the new bill rate falls to 12% in point of time. If we do not adjust the old contracts' value for time elapsed, you will show a profit of 2% on the contracts' original full nominal value. On your investment of $10 million nominal, this means a profit of $200 000 for a year, or $100 000 for six months. If this amount is subtracted from the discount price you would pay for the new 12%, you will have effectively returned to 14%.

This process could probably be repeated in the actual delivery procedure if that option was chosen, for as already mentioned, there are many deliverable grades of bills which could satisfy this contract requirement. It is quite possible that you could receive more than $10 million principal value bills at delivery at a lower discount rate if those particular instruments satisfy the clearing corporation.

There are two basic types of costs involved in this procedure. The first are the commission costs charged by your broker for his services. The second is more invisible and involves the opportunity costs lost when you placed money down on margin. This money did not earn interest during the life of the contract and its loss of earning power should undoubtedly be factored into the total returns produced by the hedge.

This general example helps illustrate the problems and choices faced by investors using the futures markets. Situations become more complex as the futures strategy becomes more complex, especially if the strategy involves arbitrage on more than one type of financial instrument. However, mechanics and strategies notwithstanding, financial futures markets pose larger questions which cannot be addressed or answered at a trading floor level. Several of these questions should be posed in general terms since they raise issues about the benefits and drawbacks of interest-rate trading.

ECONOMICS OF FUTURES TRADING

Many claims can be, and are, made concerning the ultimate benefits of futures trading. Initially, we discussed the advantages of hedging from the investor's perspective only but there are other market participants who derive benefit from the markets. Perhaps foremost among these are the dealers in debt securities in the USA who form the professional market-making side of the securities business, whether it be in corporate bonds or government and agency instruments.

This network of over-the-counter dealers is the essential structure of bond distribution. In gross terms, this community has the most to lose if erratic swings occur in interest-rate markets. At any given time, the major dealers may have several billion dollars of bond inventory among them, both of primary and secondary issues. Any precipitous rate move-ments could cause the network to suffer losses, resulting in serious consequences for the financial system as a whole.

For example, if a securities dealer suffers realised losses at the hands of the yield curve, the loss cannot simply be isolated. It may have a ripple effect if the dealer fails to deliver to other firms/banks with which it trades or has securities arrangements. Since commercial banks are large dealers in government securities, regardless of locale or nationality, losses are likely to affect earnings and perhaps the capital base of the institution. Losses in bond, money market, and foreign currency trading are similar to defaults in the Euromarket where the effect can be felt in interbank deposits.[3]

Both aspects of futures trading can aid in developing liquidity in the cash market. On a relatively simple level, the ability to mitigate risk by financial institutions can be of benefit to both the secondary markets and the new issues markets. But on a higher and more complex level, futures markets have the potential to make the cash markets increasingly efficient through arbitrage or other cross-influences.

Imagine for a moment a yield curve, in a positive slope, with bond yields as follows:

5 years	13.00%
6 years	13.15%
7 years	13.32%
8 years	13.49%
9 years	13.67%
10 years	13.39%
12 years	14.00%

According to the slope, although the differentials between maturity dates are not exactly incremental, the ten-year bond is over-priced; that is, its yield is too low, or off the curve. A trader, recognising this, may be willing to short it in anticipa-tion of its price falling to a proper level.

In order to sell that issue short several assumptions would have to be made. First it would be necessary to assume that

the curve would keep its current slope and that the differentials between maturity dates were reflective of market
conditions and expectations. Second, the trader would need
to know why the ten-year bond is too expensive. But
assuming that these issues can be resolved, it may be decided
to short the ten-year bond, or 'butterfly the yield curve'.[4]

This could be accomplished by selling short an actual
ten-year cash bond or by shorting the ten-year bond future.
The latter course of action is usually more expedient in this
instance because the precise contract exists and thereby
avoids delivery problems and higher execution costs.

Futures markets, like share options markets, also have
their drawbacks and present an economic problem of potentially significant proportions which has yet to be fully realised
in practice. This has to do with the relationship between the
amount of underlying securities outstanding *vis-à-vis* the
amount of open interest outstanding against them.[5]

This relationship is perhaps best stated in the phrase 'the
futures market leads the cash market'. This implies that when
futures prices rise or fall, cash prices are apt to follow because
of the subsequent arbitrage between the markets. Obviously,
the cash market also leads the futures market. The problem
lying beneath this process takes this situation to the ultimate
degree whereby the number of contracts outstanding (in gross
nominal terms) exceeds the total outstanding nominal capitalisation of the debt securities deliverable against it. Therefore,
a significant short on long futures position is likely to affect
the treasury securities in question.

This possibility is not as far-fetched as it sounds since it has
already occurred in the American share options market. The
possibility of it happening in the futures market is quite
plausible because of the high level of gearing present. Table
1.3 sets out the outstanding open interest on the ten most
popular long-term US Treasury bonds and the open interest
against them. As one compares the numbers, the inevitable
question arises as to whether prices could be seriously
affected either by sheer demand or manipulation.

This situation provides the ultimate potential drawback to
financial futures trading. The ramifications can be far-
reaching and significant in each particular market. In foreign

Table 1.3 Bond Future Open Interest *v.* Long-term Bond
Capitalisation, end 1982

open interest	*capitalisation*
181 210 contracts* representing value of $18.121billion	$23.20 billion†

* In all delivery months, $100 000 contracts
† Representing 7 issues with coupons in excess of 10%

exchange futures, it could potentially cause a run on a currency but this is not likely due to the traditional forward markets hold on the large volume of foreign exchange trading. However, in the US Treasury bill sector it could be quite serious. Any abnormal price movements in bills can affect the Treasury department's debt management ability by impacting the cost of borrowing. In the bond sector, an aberration in demand can affect the debt ceiling, a level which still has to be ratified by congress. A temporary freeze on the issuance of further debt plus heightened pressures from the futures market at the same time could throw the long end of the yield curve into confusion and again seriously affect subsequent costs of borrowing both to governmental and non-governmental borrowers alike.

The fact that futures hedging helps eliminate risk should not be confused with the notion that more risk can therefore be assumed simply because there now exists a means to mitigate it. In more technical language, the availability of hedging does not necessarily imply a shift in investors' preference or indifference levels. There is no reason to suspect that investors will become attracted to higher risk, high yielding instruments simply for this reason. As we have already seen, hedging a high yielding instrument with a better quality lower yielding one presents the investor with a wide spread of basis risk which cannot be hedged. Therefore it would not be correct to assume that investors' behaviour will be altered by access to hedging instruments; investors will continue to assume risk or be risk averse for fundamental rather than technical considerations.

Perhaps the most important reason for not assuming additional risk is still the one fundamental which tends to be occasionally lost in the maze of futures terminology and strategies: credit risk cannot be hedged. A marginal basis risk, the result of a cross-hedge, can become quite substantial if the reputation of the borrower falters. There certainly is no protection against this possibility for the investor. The only consolation holders of fixed income instruments have if their holdings fall sharply in credit rating terms is that their prices will probably stabilise after a precipitous fall as speculative investors begin to buy the instruments as outright speculative investments. But this type of predatory elasticity will not normally return the instrument to its original yield level.

However one views financial futures, there is no denying their increasing prominence on the international financial landscape. Regardless of arguments put forth by proponents and detractors alike, recent monetary history has ensured them of a permanent place in the financial markets. Unlike the cash markets, whose structures necessarily suggest an obvious single dimension, the markets are perhaps the best single financial indicator of attitudes concerning the future.

NOTES

1. This yield reflection is not properly known as a yield curve but as a 'strip' curve. More will be said about this in Chapters 3 and 4.
2. See J. R. Hicks, *Value and Capital* (Oxford University Press, 1978) ch. 3, and J. M. Keynes, *A Treatise on Money* (London: Macmillan, 1936) vol. 2.
3. This is referred to as a 'tiering' phenomenon. If a bank suffers real or expected losses, the rate at which it can attract funds for deposit will have to rise as other wholesale institutions in the interbank market demand more return for their risk placed with it. In extreme cases, other dealers will close off the bank's access to the market entirely.
4. The term 'butterfly' refers to the configuration of the three yields in question. In this case, the body of the butterfly is the anomaly and will be sold.

5. The amount of open interest on a position versus the outstanding cash position is also a matter of concern in the listed share options markets. See, for example, C. R. Geisst, *A Guide to the Financial Markets* (London: Macmillan, 1982) ch. 6.

2 Currency Futures

When Chicago's International Monetary Market (IMM) launched currency futures trading in 1972, forward exchange markets had already been in existence for a century.[1] Many of the 'grey beards' in the well-established forward market regarded the new entry with some scorn. How could this new currency market, which shared a floor with the pork belly and soyabean pits, situated in the depths of the mid-West, hope to compete with the highly liquid conventional market?

Yet the first decade of the IMM's existence has shown that currency futures trading on the IMM is no gimmick designed by 'currency rookies' in the commodity pits. Rather, the IMM has been successful in launching an entirely new method of trading currencies, which has been attractive relative to the conventional method of the forward exchange markets to a large number of transactors in foreign exchange. In particular, the innovation of the currency futures market has enabled the smaller-sized customer to have his orders fulfilled under highly competitive conditions, a privilege denied him in the conventional forward exchange market.

The IMM was favoured by luck in the early days of its existence. The new market was founded in the uneasy period of exchange-rate stability that followed the Smithsonian Agreement of December 1971 under which the advanced countries committed themselves to limit the fluctuation of their currencies one against another. Against the background of only small daily movements in exchange rates, the prospects for the new market did not look bright. The hedging and speculative business which the IMM hoped to attract thrives on exchange-rate instability, not stability. But then in the

31

summer of 1972 the British pound became the first major currency to break loose from its Smithsonian parity and float in the foreign exchange market. Several months later, in early 1973, the US dollar was floated and the age of generalised floating had begun. Turnover in the currency futures market soared.

Whilst the IMM has been successful in promoting currency futures to an important segment of the trading public, it would be absurd to pretend that the IMM will ever account for more than a small proportion of total foreign exchange business. If floor space was expanded sustantially to accommodate more traders, and hence more business, the open outcry method of transacting (a type of auction) which is the essence of futures trading would become much less efficient, and the IMM's comparative advantages (from the viewpoint of certain transactors) would dwindle.

THE OPEN OUTCRY

The organisation of trading in the currency futures market is entirely similar to that of trading in commodity futures markets. All orders to buy or sell must be transmitted to the trading floor, and must be made public there. In effect, every order gives rise to an auction on the floor. The method of trading is described as one of open outcry. To illustrate how open outcry trading occurs, consider the dollar/mark futures market, where the standard contract traded on the IMM is for DM 125,000 size. Mr K, an outside speculator (i.e. not being a member of the exchange and therefore unable to execute orders in person on the floor of the exchange) decides to go long on Deutsche marks for 20 contracts. A commission broker (i.e. a member of the exchange whose main business is taking orders from the outside public and executing these on the floor) is contacted and asked about the current rate quoted on the floor for $/DMs. The commission broker, Mr C, can given an indication only, as the actual price which will be obtained depends on trading conditions when the order is auctioned on the floor. Often C will choose for indication purposes the two-way price (bid and offer) quoted by 'market-makers' on the exchange floor (see below). Suppose the illustrative quote is 0.4452–4 $/DM. K can then give a purchase order to C in one of two principal forms:

1. *Market-order*; C is instructed to buy 20 contracts on the best terms available, and with no undue delay.
2. *Limit-order*; C is instructed to buy 20 contracts, but at a price of no higher than a given maximum, say 0.4454 $/DM. In giving a limit-order, K may want to protect himself against the risk of the market having run ahead by the time the order reaches the floor, or of buying during a period when there is a transitory shortage of mark sellers. He cannot be sure that the limit-order will be executed, and the average time of execution is greater for limit-orders than for market-orders. He has a good chance, though, of obtaining a keener price with a limit-order than with a market-order.

Other variants of the two basic types of orders can be found. Many of the variations concern the length of time for which the order is valid, and whether it must be completed all at once, or whether it may be filled in chunks. For example, K may give a 'fill or kill' order, meaning that C must have the entire bid for 20 contracts put on the floor at once, and if it is not satisfied fully by a counterparty on the other side, he must withdraw it. In the description that follows, we consider the more normal types of orders, which may be matched by several deals on the floor that do not have to occur simultaneously, although as close together as possible. Note that under an ordinary limit-order it would be possible for C to report back to K that he had managed to buy 10 but not 20 contracts at $/DM 0.4454.

C, having received the order from K, telephones the order immediately to the floor of the exchange; a 'runner' takes the order from the phone-in point to the floor broker employed by C in the trading pit. On the order's arrival at the phone-in point, the piece of paper on which it is carried to the pit is time-stamped; on US futures exchanges, orders are bracketed into half-hour periods for the purpose of time-stamping. Sometimes if the volume of business coming to C is high, he may give some orders to independent floor brokers (self-employed) who execute the orders on C's behalf for a fixed fee (around $2 per contract).

On receipt of the order, the floor broker, Mr A, should proceed to execute it as quickly as possible, except where it has a limit price attached which is now quite far removed from the range of prices being quoted. In our example, on receiving the order (assume this to be a market-order) to buy 20 Deutsche mark contracts, Mr A bids for 20 contracts, making a bid-quote probably somewhat keener (i.e. less $s/DM) than the last quoted price. As illustrated, A may be aware that Deutsche marks have recently been offered at 0.4453 $/DM and tries bidding for 20 Deutsche mark contracts at $/DM 0.4452. The bid is submitted on the floor by open outcry – this usually means that hand signals are used to indicate a buyer of 20 mark contracts at the given price. Now it may be that another floor broker, Mr B, has almost simultaneously received an order to sell 10 mark contracts. Mr B makes a hand signal showing him to be an offerer of 10 mark contracts at say, $/DM 0.4453. If no one else on the floor is immediately interested in bidding or offering for marks within the range of $/DM 0.4452–3, then it is likely that Messrs A and B would agree to conclude a deal for 10 contracts at an 'in between' price of say, $/DM 0.4452½. Agreement is noted by an exchange official, and cards are filled in and time-stamped with reference made on them to the underlying customer order.[2] Mr B's order is now completed; it is endorsed on the back, with details of the transaction, then time-stamped and sent by the runners to the telephone area, where notification is sent to the relevant commission broker.

Mr A has so far succeeded in buying only 10 out of the required 20 contracts for his client. If another seller of marks does not emerge quickly, it may be necessary to approach one of those independent floor traders who maintain two-way quotes (they do this by using both hands, one palm towards them and one palm away, indicating that they are both bidding for and offering marks). This type of independent floor trader (called a 'market-maker') hopes to earn income from providing liquidity; with a gross income equalling the cumulative difference between the rate at which marks are bought and sold. The 'bid' and 'offer' rates, quoted simultaneously, are separated by a small margin. For example, Mr M – a market-maker – may currently have a two-way quote of $/DM 0.4452–4; then Mr B might conclude an order by buying 10 Deutsche mark contracts from Mr M at $/DM 0.4454. It is out of the bid-offer spread that Mr M earns the income which provides a return for the risk of inventory holding (the market-maker must assume inventory positions in the course of his trading), for the price of his seat, and which compensates him for leisure forgone or for income forgone from other occupations. As Mr M gains a reputation for using both hands, other floor traders know that it is worth their while looking his way even when activity is brisk and the floor crowded with many bids and offers being made simultaneously; the reputation should boost his trading volume. If, in contrast, M quoted only intermittently on his own account, in active business conditions many traders might not go out of their way to check whether Mr M was now 'in the market' and had an attractive quote. In busy conditions Mr M himself cannot be aware of all bids and offers being made concurrently, and respond to them in a one-handed fashion. If there was merely a response with one hand to bids or offers that arose, a lot of potential business would pass him by. In sum, the potential extra business gained by Mr M using two hands rather than one is likely to increase with the volume of business on the trading floor.

Sometimes there will be no immediate counterpart at all to Mr A (excluding market-maker floor traders); furthermore, Mr A may find that there are several other floor traders also bidding for marks. It is in this situation that those independent floor traders called 'scalpers' would come to the fore. Seeing that there is an excess demand for marks, the scalpers would be willing to take a short position in marks themselves, and offer marks at a somewhat higher price than the last quoted rate, anticipating that the shortage is transitory, and that soon a cluster of sell orders for marks will come to the floor; at that time, the scalper would hope to be able to buy marks to close his short position at a cheaper price than that at which the position was opened. Market-makers' function overlaps that of scalpers; Mr M, on seeing a large group of buy orders for marks, would raise his quote from say 0.4452–4 to

0.4452½–4½ \$/DM. The floor brokers bidding for marks would conclude deals with scalpers and market-makers at 0.4454½ \$/DM. Every scalper is not a market-maker; many scalpers maintain only one-way quotes.

The rules of a commodity and currency futures exchange prevent a commission broker satisfying an order by merely taking an opposite position himself through his agent on the exchange floor. For example, if there were no immediate offers of Deutsche marks the commission broker, or his agent, might see advantage in supplying marks to his customer at say, \$/DM 0.4454½, so going short in marks; but the exchange rules prevent a commission broker (or his agent on the floor) dealing with his customer in this way. Any order received must be presented on the floor of the exchange for all to see; and one safeguard for the customer that this will be done is the rule described. For if the broker could deal directly with the customer, there would be scope for dishonesty; the broker could sell Deutsche marks to his customer at a rate inferior to that which could have been obtained through open auction.

In principle, the open outcry method of trading provides a very competitive framework in which the customer's order can be fulfilled, and this feature is what makes currency futures markets relatively attractive to the smaller customer, who often does not enjoy competitive access to the conventional forward market. But a note of caution should be sounded. Dishonest practices are possible on the exchange floor which impede the forces of competition producing the keenest possible quote for the customer.

1. *Collusion*: If a floor broker, Mr A, receives a very large purchase order for Deutsche marks (say, 100 contracts), he realises that as soon as he signals the bid in the pit, the price of the Deutsche mark will move up from this last recorded level, as scalpers must be 'enticed' to assume the necessary inventory position. He may collude with another floor trader, Mr E, using some secret gesture to indicate that he has just received a large order to buy marks; then Mr E could buy marks ahead of Mr A making his bid public, and make a profit from selling marks to Mr A's client. A reciprocal agreement would exist presumably whereby Mr A would do similar

services for Mr E when the opportunity arises. The outside trader (not a party to the collusion) loses from the existence of collusive agreements; in the example, a seller of Deutsche marks in the interval of time between Mr A receiving the buy order and his placing it in the pit for auction would receive an artificially low price (in dollars); buyers of marks during that period would benefit from the collusion, but a large proportion of the counterpart purchases would be made by Mr E, an active instigator of the collusion.

2. *Order priority*. Mr A, on receiving an order to buy 20 contracts in Deutsche marks, may believe that the price of DMs is moving up (on very short-term considerations). It may be that some favourable news for the Deutsche mark has just been released. Mr A may then purchase marks on his own account first, obtaining the keenest possible terms available, and afterwards purchase marks to fulfil the customer's order, presumably on less favourable terms. Given that orders for the purpose of time-stamping are bracketed into half-hour periods, there is no simple method for the exchange authorities to prevent this type of abuse occurring over short periods of time.[3]

3. *Information-trading*. When a non-member gives his order to a commission broker, he realises that the order will not be executed immediately because of the time-delay in transmitting the order to the floor of the exchange. The time-delay exposes the outside trader (non-member) to the risk that new information may come in during the brief intervening period that would have made him reluctant to place the order now in process. This risk is most serious for the trader who has given a limit-order. In the earlier example, suppose the trader had given a limit-order to buy 20 mark contracts at $/DM 0.4454 or better (when the indicated price was $/DM 0.4453–5): by giving such a limit-order he hopes that it will be executed at a time when there is a transitory bunching of sale orders for marks, rather than at a time when no sellers of marks are around so that a premium price would have to be paid to entice the scalpers into action. But the strategy behind the limit-order can backfire. For suppose that no sooner had the limit-order been placed, than a piece of news was released which was bearish for the mark. The price

of the mark (the $/DM rate) would drop and the limit-order would be easily fulfilled. However, if instantaneous communication between the customer and the floor broker had been possible, the customer would either have withdrawn his outstanding limit-order before it could be executed, or have lowered the limit (expressed in terms of the $/DM rate) at which he was prepared to purchase marks. Because instantaneous communication is not possible, the customer becomes a buyer of marks at a price higher than that which he would now willingly pay.

The 'involuntary' execution of limit-orders which occurs just after the release of new important information is a source of profit to independent floor traders. They realise that new information will bring forth a burst of limit-orders, and so they can transact at a price which does not yet fully reflect the changed circumstances. In the example, independent traders would be sellers of marks, satisfying the cluster of bids for marks arising out of limit-orders. It is not just the customer who has given the limit-order to purchase marks that loses, it is also those customers who have given market-orders to buy marks; they will buy marks at a somewhat inflated price in the new circumstances, as it is at first supported by the burst of limit-orders. As counterbalance, however, sellers of marks who have given a market-order rather than a limit-order would obtain a favourable price, given the new circumstances. On a net basis, it is the limit-order customers who fuel the profits of the floor traders at a time of new information appearing.

CURRENCY FUTURES CONTRACTS[4]

On Chicago's IMM, listed currency futures contracts include those in Deutsche marks, Swiss francs, British pounds, Japanese yen, Canadian dollars, French francs, Dutch guilders and Mexican pesos. The most active contracts are the first five mentioned. Contract sizes and delivery dates are standardised, and all trading is *vis-à-vis* the US dollar. The size of a unit contract in each of the active currencies, £25 000; C$100 000; Swiss francs 125 000; DM 125 000;

Yen 12 500 000. In each currency, there is a maximum of nine delivery dates traded – the third Wednesday of January, March, April, June, July, September, October, December and of the spot month. Dealing in a particular contract (e.g. June pounds) terminates on the second business day immediately preceding the third Wednesday of the contract month. Delivery of the currency bought (against dollars) is made into a bank to an account as designated by the buyer; the bank specified must be in the country of issue of the currency (e.g. British pounds purchased must be delivered into an account within Britain).

All currency futures contracts (like commodity futures contracts) have as one party the Clearing Corporation. For example, customer K, having had the marks purchased, would find that the other side to the contract (the person with the obligation to sell marks) would be the Chicago Clearing Corporation. Thus the Clearing Corporation stands behind all contracts. It is pertinent thereby to ask what is the credit status of the Corporation, and how without actively participating in any trade it becomes the counterpart to each contract.

The Clearing Corporation has as its participants those members of the IMM, with sufficiently large capital resources to satisfy the strict financial requirements, who see financial advantage from participation. Because the Clearing Corporation stands behind all contracts its ultimate capital resources, which could be drawn on, influence the credit risks of IMM contracts. Clearing members are assessable where one of them fails and cash is required to honour the contracts into which his customers have entered. Potential economic advantage from being a clearing corporation participant – i.e. a clearing member of the IMM – comes from the collection of clearing fees and from the practice of margin collection. A clearing member collects margins from all customers (whether members or not) who have dealt through him and who have open positions. But the clearing member himself needs deposit margin with the Clearing Corporation only on the net value of open positions which he or his customers are holding now. A non-clearing member must clear all positions through a clearing member (see below) and is not allowed to net positions of his clients for the purpose of calculating what margin he is due to put with the clearing member.

To see how the Clearing Corporation enters as a party to each contract, let us return to the process of auction by open outcry. Suppose floor trader Mr A buys (on behalf of his client, Mr K) 20 mark contracts from floor trader Mr B (who is a scalper operating for his own account) where both A and B are non-clearing members of the IMM. Both Mr A and Mr B must each have a clearing account with a clearing member, let us say F and G respectively. Then A's purchase of marks is registered by the IMM official as attributable to F as clearer; similarly B's sale of marks is attributed to G as clearer. F and G guarantee contract performance by A and B respectively. As a result of the transaction, F increases its long position in marks with the Clearing Corporation; simultaneously G increases its short position in marks with the Clearing Corporation. At the end of each day, the position of the Clearing Corporation with each member is calculated (over-all the Clearing Corporation has zero position in each currency, but it can have substantial net positions with individual members), and a margin requirement for each member is calculated.

Profits and losses on outstanding contracts are calculated and payable daily. For example, suppose F has a long position in 1000 Deutsche mark contracts with the Clearing Corporation, where this long position has built up recently; then the mark rises suddenly against the US dollar. A profit would be calculated on F's position, and this would be payable immediately, probably being deducted from any additional net margin requirement. The clearing members at the end of each day act in similar fashion *vis-à-vis* their own customers as the Clearing Corporation *vis-à-vis* themselves. For instance, F advises each member client of the net profit which his position has earned during the past day, and credits (or debits, if a loss) the amount to his account, deducting this from any new net margin payable; F acts in a similar fashion with respect to non-member clients.

Efficiency in margin collection is crucial to promoting the creditworthiness of IMM contracts. If commission broker A was slow in his collection of margins, and the exchange rate moved by a large amount, he might find that he had insufficient funds to meet the margin call made by clearing member F at the end of the day. Liquidity problems for A and its customers may spill over into creating liquidity problems for F. If F could no longer meet its commitments, the Clearing Corporation would draw on financial resources of its other members to honour them. It is highly unlikely that the fairly mild daily swings in currency rates could engender a liquidity crisis for the Clearing Corporation; the more likely crisis centre in the futures market would be the pits trading commodities subject to highly unstable price conditions. In the heady days of the gold boom of late 1979 and early 1980, rumours circulated about possible credit difficulties of some clearing houses on US commodity futures markets. The wild gyrations of the gold price led to large margin calls being made by brokers; these sometimes could not be met, leading the broker to liquidate his customer's position; and liquidation could inflict a loss on the customer greater than the net margin which he had deposited. A large number of such net deficiencies could bankrupt the broker, and in turn create a liquidity problem for some clearing members.

The currency futures market in Chicago has carried over the practice of imposing daily limits on price movements, from the commodity futures exchanges. The purpose of limit rules is to give members 'breathing space' in which to collect margins following a large price movement, rather than waiting till the end of a normal trading day, when time would be limited to deal with possible problems of collection from certain customers. Under the limit rule, trading ceases if the price moves more than a given amount from the previous day's close. Trading is permitted to occur only in the range between yesterday's closing price and the limit prices in both directions. On the day following a trading stop, the limit price is adjusted by a given amount, and normally trading would start again within the expanded range. If not, then the limit price would be adjusted further on the third day. By the fifth day, if no trading has yet resumed, all limits are removed. But before the reader becomes impressed by the genesis tone of these limit rules, it should be stressed that they have been activated only for the Mexican peso; the active currencies have never swung by enough in one day to trigger an application of the limit rule.

Clearing members also act as paying agents in the effecting of physical delivery under futures contracts. About 3% of currency futures contracts are not closed out before maturity (i.e. the second business day preceding the third Wednesday of the contract month). Where contracts are closed out before maturity, they are struck off the current register of the Clearing Corporation. For example, if customer K takes first a long position in a Deutsche mark contract, then closes it out by taking an equal short position in a Deutsche mark contract, K's broker, Mr C, notifies his clearer, Mr F, that two contracts which he has cleared have now cancelled each other out; there is of course no margin requirement due on such mutually offsetting positions attributable to one customer. The procedure for closing out orders does effectively constrain the customer to deal through the same broker in both the opening and closing transaction. All contracts on the clearing house's register at the close of business on the last trading day (for this particular contract) give rise to a physical delivery of currency. All those with outstanding positions on the last trading day (against which deliveries are now to be made) make one final daily payment (or receive one final payment from), as distinct from payment due against delivery, to the clearing house, based on the difference between the closing price on the penultimate and on the final day of the contract's life. Thus if the closing dollar/mark rate has fallen on the last day, then someone carrying a long position in Deutsche marks over to the delivery stage will make a payment to the Clearing House equal to the loss made. The purchase price billed for the marks bought is the closing price on the last day of trading. But in calculating the effective cost of the marks, the trader would subtract (add) the daily profits (losses) he had been paid by the clearing house as the mark had appreciated (depreciated) over the lifetime of the contract: the effective cost of the marks should be close to the futures price at which the deal was initially struck; a small difference is possible though due to an accumulation of interest on cash received during the contract's life.

Let us take the example of a mark futures contract to demonstrate the delivery procedure. The clearing member representing a customer with a long position in marks must present a 'buyer's delivery commitment' to the clearing house no later than 12.00 noon on the last day of trading. By 1.00 p.m. the clearing member must deposit to the account of the Clearing Corporation, in a bank designated by it, the dollar amount due against purchase of the marks. The buyer of marks specifies into which account at which bank in Germany he wishes the marks to be paid. The clearing member representing a customer selling marks must similarly present to the clearing house by 12.00 noon on the last day of trading a Seller's Delivery Commitment. The clearing house, having received the relevant Sellers' and Buyers' Delivery Commitments, matches these, assigning a buyer to each seller (this is done on a net basis between clearing members). The seller's clearing member, upon receiving a Buyer's Delivery Commitment, instructs its bank to contact and follow the instructions of the buyer's clearing member regarding the bank and the name of the account to which the delivery of marks is to be made. The bank designated by the seller's clearing member gives written notice to the IMM upon completion of delivery instructions (i.e. it confirms delivery of the marks). On receipt of this notification, the clearing house must transfer promptly the dollar funds previously deposited by the buyer's clearing member to the account of the seller's clearing member.

COMPARATIVE ADVANTAGES OF THE CURRENCY FORWARD AND FUTURES MARKETS

The traditional forward exchange market, in contrast to the currency futures market, is decentralised. For each currency several large banks make a market, almost always *vis-à-vis* the US dollar. Customers have direct access to at least one market-maker in the forward exchange market, and so can obtain a direct quote and complete their deal instantaneously. This contrasts with the currency futures market, where a transactor either gives a market-order, thereby accepting some uncertainty as to price, or gives a limit-order, thereby accepting some uncertainty as to whether his order will be completed. In the currency forward market, if a customer asks for a quote from his bank, the bank is obliged to deal on the basis of the quote up to a conventionally fixed maximum (around $10 million) so long as the customer has established the necessary credit arrangements (both spot and forward exchange transactions impose a credit risk on the bank, due to the possibility of the customer defaulting).

It is normal for a customer to ask his bank for a two-way quote (bid and offer) without revealing whether he is a buyer or seller of the currency in question: this provides the customer with some protection against a very uncompetitive quote being made, even where he does not have much scope to shop around for alternative quotes from other banks. For suppose the customer is a buyer of marks; if the bank knows this then it can quote $/DM bid and offer rates somewhat more favourable to the seller of marks and less favourable to the buyer of marks than the market 'average quote', and yet have no fear that the customer will accept its cheap offer of dollars. It could operate in reverse fashion with a customer who had revealed an intention to sell marks, and quote a $/DM rate that was favourable to the buyer of marks and unfavourable to the seller of marks, knowing that the favourable side of the offer would not be taken up. Thus where the customer reveals his intentions, the quoting of an impressively low spread between bid and offer rates by the bank is no protection against a very poor rate being offered. Where the bank does not know the customer's intention, the constraint of having to keep the bid-offer spread to a reasonable level affords some protection against a very uncompetitive rate being made.

But many bank-customer relationships are such that the bank would be able to guess in which direction his customer intends to deal even when this is not stated. For instance, a customer which is a small import agent would find it difficult to disguise from its banker its intention to buy rather than sell foreign currency. A large import agent with accepted credit limits at several banks should be able to obtain competitive terms even though each bank knows its intended direction of business, because they are aware that the customer can obtain alternative quotes elsewhere. The small customer has no such protection. Even where the small customer's direction of business is not known by the bank, it does not have competitive access to the market. The small customer might be a buyer of marks, yet its bank could currently have an excess short position in marks; then the bank would make a relatively expensive rate for buying marks. The small customer with no other credit relationships cannot shop around to obtain a keener sale price for marks elsewhere. It is the small customer who stands to gain most from the currency futures market system of open outcry, which provides for competitive fulfilment of orders, for he is most deprived of the benefits of competition in the traditional forward exchange market. As against the gain of competitive order fulfilment, the customer must offset the disadvantage of non-instaneous fulfilment and the associated hazards of market- and limit-orders.

The market-maker on the floor of the currency futures market has an important advantage relative to his counterpart in the forward market. He can see how other marketmakers and floor traders react to a new piece of information; further he can see the overall flow of business to the trading floor, and how it is biased between buy and sell orders, rather than being subject to some degree of isolation as is the market-maker in the forward market. Suppose news comes to the market of a larger than expected trade surplus in Germany for the latest reporting month. Any market-maker can look round to see how other floor traders have adjusted their bids or offers, and change his accordingly. In contrast, in the forward market, the foreign exchange manager at bank A does not know immediately how managers at other banks have adjusted their quotes. For example, bank A may move its mark/dollar quote from 2.2535–45 to 2.2505–15; but simultaneously bank B may move its quote from 2.2536–46 to 2.2514–24. These adjustments imply that bank B believes that the news will be received less bullishly in the market than does A. As a result of the disparity of quotes, B would find itself concluding an extraordinary number of mark sales at DM/$ 2.2514 whilst A would conclude an extraordinary number of mark purchases at DM/$ 2.2515. The average difference in the market between buying and selling prices at which transactions are effected would shrink, causing an aggregate loss of income to market-makers. Growing imbalance in opposite directions of A and B's inventory would cause them to bring their quotes together. The market-maker who had best judged the market response would make least, and possible zero, subsequent adjustment of quote. Occasionally it has been alleged that large banks in a particular currency have conspired to prevent a dispersion of quotes developing after new information is released. In this way aggregate market-making profits are not eroded and risk exposure should be reduced, in the wake of an important news release.

The market-maker in the forward market becomes aware of changing market sentiment only as he can detect it from the business reaching him and the normal lines of communication with foreign exchange brokers. Suppose he has just concluded two large sales of Deutsche marks, with there having been no in between purchase of marks. He does not know whether the succession of two large mark sales is indicative of a change towards bearishness in market sentiment or merely due to chance; buy and sell orders arrive in a stochastic fashion, and bunching together of deals in one direction may occur without signifying any overall change in market sentiment. If a market-maker could see the direction of business that had come to all other market-makers during the recent past, he would be better able to determine whether a genuine change in sentiment had occurred; if other market-makers also had been net sellers of marks over the most recent past, then there would be a higher probability (most likely far short of 100%) that a change in market sentiment had occurred than was noticeable from one market-maker's business alone.

Thus the decentralisation of the forward exchange market blunts the immediate reaction of market quotes to a change in market sentiment, as market-makers there are less well placed than in the IMM to distinguish shifts in general market direction from random variations in business coming to themselves. A market-maker in a decentralised market is likely to be a loser during the immediate aftermath of a change in market direction; he protects his overall revenue against these periodic losses (plus slimmed profits on average immediately after new important information) by quoting a wider-than-otherwise bid-offer spread at all times. The infrequent transactor in foreign exchange who believes it is unlikely that he will be able to hit one of the periods when market-makers in general are losers, or take advantage of the dispersion of quotes in the immediate aftermath of new information (due to his lack of credit arrangements with competing market-makers), would presumably be biased towards trading in the currency futures rather than forward market. Market-makers on the IMM do not have to build a margin into their bid-offer spread to cover the losses made following a change in market sentiment and to compensate for the increased risk borne when new important information is released. Nor does the currency futures market, like the currency forward market, have to bear the heavy costs of brokerage and other channels of inter-market-maker communication. In the IMM, the market-maker, or any floor trader, can lay off positions simply by open outcry. In the centralised currency futures market, there is a significantly lower proportion of business between dealers themselves and a higher proportion between ultimate non-dealer customers than is true for the decentralised forward market (where the counterpart to the floor trader is the bank as market-maker).

IMM members are in general less able to appraise the creditworthiness of their clients than are banks, and this puts them at some disadvantage in trading currencies. For example, one central feature of IMM organisation is the taking of margins from customers against all open positions. To some extent margins are tailored to the credit risk of the client; the IMM itself sets only minimum margin requirements. But many commission brokers levy above minimum margin requirements from customers of questionable credit status. Margin requirements may be satisfied by the depositing of T-bills or cash; even where T-bills are placed some loss of earnings is likely to be experienced by the client relative to what could have been earned on freely disposable funds. The IMM, in setting margin rules, cannot take into account the refinements of credit relationships that a bank can. For example, an importing company in Britain reduces the risk to

which its overall profit is exposed by buying foreign currency
forward. If it bought forward the currency from its own bank
no margin would be required; indeed the bank's loans
outstanding to the company would have been reduced in risk.
But if the company deals with an IMM member, the latter
perceives an increase of its risk-bearing by dealing with the
company, despite the overall riskiness of the company having
decreased; the need for a margin payment arises from the
splitting of the company's foreign exchange business from its
normal credit business.

The difficulty encountered by an IMM member in appraising the creditworthiness of his client handicaps the procedure
for physical delivery of currency, and IMM procedures are
more cumbersome here than are those of the traditional
foreign exchange market. Suppose that in the latter a bank
client has bought DM 1 million spot against dollars (i.e. for
settlement two business days ahead). The bank arranges that
the DM 1 million are credited to the account of the customer's
choosing (in Germany) and requests the customer to pay the
dollar counterpart into the bank's nominated account (in the
USA). The bank assumes some credit risk in that it pays the
marks to its customer's account *before* confirmation has been
received that dollars have been paid into its own account. Yet
where the bank has knowledge of the customer's affairs, and
the transaction falls well within his usual credit limit, the
arrangement of the spot transaction is a matter of mere
routine. The IMM member, and its clearer, are in contrast
ill-equipped to handle the credit risk associated with the spot
transaction. Thus IMM delivery rules (see p. 42) stipulate that
the buyer of marks should pay dollars into the IMM's account
two days before the delivery of marks, and that the seller of
marks does not receive his dollar funds until the clearing
house has received confirmation from the clearing member's
bank acting for the seller that the marks have been delivered.

In the currency futures market, unlike in the forward market,
the transactor can elect to forego the services of a market-
maker or scalper and hope thereby to obtain a reduction in
transaction costs in return for non-instantaneous fulfilment of
his order. He does this by placing a limit-order, instructing his

broker to sell marks for dollars only when a quote could be obtained equal to what market-makers would now bid rather than offer for marks, reflecting the emergence of a transitory bunching of buy orders for marks after a period when sell orders have been bunched. Equivalently, in the futures markets, the transactor can choose his own optimum trade-off between speed of having his order effected and amount of transaction cost incurred.

Unlike the traditional forward exchange market, the currency futures market is not equipped to handle trans-actions for odd sizes and odd dates. It would be almost impossible for a floor trader to match orders for odd sizes, and to fulfil them he would have to assume some inventory positions himself. But to allow the floor broker to fulfil a customer's order partly 'out of his own book' would run counter to an important safeguard rule of IMM organisation. Moreover, if bids and counteroffers could be expressed in a huge range of sizes the mechanics of floor trading would be greatly complicated. It is difficult to imagine how hand signals could be developed for a large range of sizes (and dates).

A bank, in quoting for forward exchange, derives an advantage from also being active in the spot, swap and deposit markets. The bank can lay off its exposure from having sold Deutsche marks three months outright forward against dollars to a customer by either buying marks forward from another customer or by buying marks spot and swapping these into dollars.[5] Further, if taking the second route, it can – as an alternative to swapping marks into dollars directly – borrow dollars and lend marks.[6] The floor trader (scalpers and market-makers) in the currency futures markets has no direct role in the deposit or swap markets, and hence his ability to dispose of inventory is more circumscribed than his forward market counterpart. This disadvantage weighs par-ticularly heavily against the futures market in long-maturity contracts: commercial interest in hedging dwindles beyond the three-month maturity range, and so does turnover in the forward markets. Yet business in the deposit and credit markets declines at a slower rate with respect to maturity than does business in the forward market; indeed, a lot of credit and deposit business is concentrated in the six-month region.

Thus in the long-term forward market, liquidity creation is highly dependent on direct access to the deposit and swap markets. The futures market, without this direct access, is severely handicapped (relative to the forward market) in quoting for long-maturity business. In the IMM, very little trading occurs in currency futures contracts beyond 3–4 months into the future. At any time, there is one maturity of contract which is traded predominantly, and this is for delivery 1–4 months ahead.

The concentration of trading on the IMM in short-maturity contracts has deterred the speculator with a long-term horizon from using the futures market. A speculator who believes that current trends in Germany's trade and capital accounts will force the mark up over the next year, but is unsure of the timing, would either buy marks forward against dollars for delivery in twelve months or buy marks forward for delivery at a nearer date with the intention of rolling over the contract at maturity for further periods up to one year ahead.[7] If he decides to buy a long-term contract, this could be effected more cheaply in the forward than in the futures market. Nor is the futures market as well equipped to handle roll-over transactions as is the traditional forward market. If the speculator buys initially a mark futures contract for delivery three months ahead, he must close out his position two days before maturity and buy a new Deutsche mark futures contract; there is a direct market in 'spread' transactions on the IMM (i.e. trading two contract months against each other) and it is fairly liquid for roll-over transactions just before maturity. But the degree of liquidity of the IMM spread market is less than in the traditional swap market where the speculator with a long position in a three-month mark forward contract can close it out two days before maturity and assume simultaneously a long position in a new three-month mark forward contract. In quoting for three-month swaps, a bank, unlike the IMM dealer in the spread market, can draw directly on the liquidity of the active three-month mark and dollar deposit markets.

Many speculators taking a medium-term view (say, around one year) on the mark against the dollar would trade neither in the forward nor in the futures market. For consider a speculator whose 'neutral' investment portfolio is a basket of international monies (invested in instruments of three months maximum maturity) weighted in given proportions. If he wishes to back a medium-term view about the mark against the dollar, he would increase the proportion of the mark and decrease the proportion of the dollar in his portfolio. Changing currency proportions by dealing in the spot market and rolling over deposits on maturity (without any further exchange transaction) should be cheaper than leaving the composition of currency deposits unchanged and rolling over forward contracts.

In the currency forward market, customers can request quotes for any date, not just standardised dates as in the currency futures market. Even so, in the forward market liquidity tends to be greatest for standard maturity dates – unbroken months ahead – rather than for broken dates; a lot of transactors in their hedging transactions deal for simple multiples of months ahead. Where a bank is asked to quote for a broken month (e.g. 3 months 10 days ahead), it would normally quote a wider spread than for an unbroken month. The bank would reckon that it would probably have to match the broken month contract with an unbroken month contract in the opposite direction, leaving itself with a small amount of forward-forward exposure. The IMM organisation does not lend towards broken month trading for the following reasons: first as with odd contract sizes, the mechanics of hand trading would become hopelessly complex; secondly, the assumption of inventory position by floor brokers would conflict with exchange rules; thirdly, even if members could trade directly with their clients, they would have less flexibility than their forward market counterparts in disposing of inventory due to their isolation from the swap and deposit markets.

The IMM, like other futures markets, has decided in favour of specifying contract maturities in terms of given dates rather than of simple multiples of a month from the present trading day. The advantage of selecting this method of standardisation is the creation of a liquid secondary market for the trading of contracts – an area where the futures market has a distinct advantage over the forward market. A trader who in March buys a June mark contract on the IMM can close out

his position at any subsequent date by instructing his broker
to sell June mark futures contracts; and at that time the June
contract will still be highly liquid and the mark sale (like the
previous purchase) can be put up for competitive auction.[8] In
contrast, the client of bank A who buys marks forward against
dollars on 15 March for delivery in three months (i.e. 15
June) is in a locked-in situation. If he wanted to close out his
position on 1 April, he would be dealing for an odd date, and
be faced with an extra large bid-offer spread. Moreover his
original contract is with bank A; therefore to close out his
position fully he must again deal with bank A. If instead he
sold marks for 15 June to another bank, he would incur extra
transaction costs on settlement, and in the interval before
settlement would be subject to some credit risk. For he would
have to deliver dollars to A and receive marks from A, whilst
receiving dollars from B and paying marks to B; in the
interval before maturity he would be subject to some small
credit risk, that one of the banks may fail. Bank A, knowing
the complications which its client would face in cancelling its
forward position by trading with another bank, could afford
to quote somewhat less competitively than on the opening leg
of the forward position. In the futures market, where all
contracts are effected with the clearing house, no such
restraint on competition exists with respect to the closing out
of positions.

Exchange deals between non-dollar currencies are handled
less flexibly in the IMM than in the forward market. For
example, consider a trader who wishes to buy Swiss francs for
a forward date against Deutsche marks. In the IMM he would
normally effect this spread transaction by giving a limit order
to his broker expressed in terms of a DM/Sfr rate; the broker
would then instruct his floor agent to try to carry out two
orders, one in the mark/dollar market and one in the Swiss
franc/dollar market, such as to satisfy the customer's limit.
The floor agent, on seeing conditions in the two markets
where he is sure the limit order can be effected, would
undertake the two transactions; before proceeding to action,
the indicative cross-rate must show some safety margin over
the limit set by the customer, in case rates should move
slightly against him during the short interval of time needed to

effect the two deals. As a rule, the floor agent will effect first the deal in the less liquid of the two markets, so minimising the time between the two deals and so the risk of the combined Swiss franc/mark rate having slipped beyond the customer's limit. Because the floor agent satisfies the limit-order by dealing in the second market as quickly as possible after the first, he will often make use of the services of two-way traders (market-makers) in the second.

Unlike for a simple transaction in one currency futures market, setting a limit-order for a spread transaction (e.g. franc/marks) does not allow the customer to dispense altogether with the services of market-makers. Yet despite the probable use of market-making services in one of the two markets, the customer cannot be sure that his franc/mark order will be successfully completed; if the order is large, the customer may find that it has been partially but not completely filled. Market-orders are rarely given in spread business, for they exert no discipline on the commission broker and his agent to operate in the two markets as closely together in time as possible and to the customer's maximum advantage. Unlike when a customer gives a simple market-order (to be fulfilled in one market only), when he gives a spread order the efficiency of its fulfilment depends very much on the skill of the floor broker, and the customer is less protected by the open outcry system against the floor broker being sloppy or dishonest. Monitoring by exchange officials of possible collusion between floor traders with respect to spread dealing (e.g. in marks against francs) cannot be as strict as the monitoring of simple deals involving one market only: even if an IMM official could point to a franc/dollar and mark/dollar rate that were registered close together in time and at which a better franc/mark rate (than that which was actually obtained) could have been obtained for a customer, the floor broker could argue that the two dollar rates had not been available simultaneously.

In the forward exchange market, an instantaneous quote in mark/francs can be obtained directly from a bank. Usually the bank will simply combine its mark/dollar and franc/dollar quotes to produce its franc/mark quote, with the bid-offer spread on the latter being calculated automatically as if two transactions were in fact carried out. But unlike in the futures market, the effecting of the franc/mark deal requires no extra skill or effort on the part of the bank; the bank does not have to juggle in two markets simultaneously. The customer is not subject in any greater degree to bank inefficiency in concluding franc/mark business than franc/dollar or mark/dollar business. Whereas the IMM broker charges somewhat more commission on a spread order than on a straight order, the costs (excluding bid-offer spread) are no greater in the forward market of effecting a deal between two non-dollar currencies than between the US dollar and another currency. Moreover, some banks (in Switzerland only) enjoy sufficient business in franc/marks to justify quoting a keener bid-offer spread on franc/marks than could be obtained by putting together a franc/dollar and mark/dollar quote. Where a trader has direct access to such a bank, he is likely to find spread dealing between francs and marks on the IMM especially unattractive.

ARBITRAGE BETWEEN THE FORWARD AND FUTURES MARKET

Quotes in the IMM currency futures and the forward market are held closely together by the operation of arbitrageurs. Indeed, the possibility of arbitrage guarantees that the futures market remains liquid, albeit sometimes to a considerably lower degree than the forward market. Suppose a large sale order of Deutsche marks comes to the market floor (on the IMM); the dollar/mark rate at which scalpers are ready to bid for the marks may be so low that an arbitrageur could profit from out-bidding the scalpers and arranging almost simultaneously to sell the marks in the interbank forward exchange market. Thus the possibility of arbitrage prevents large orders in the IMM causing large swings of prices there.

The organisers of the IMM have realised the important role which forward-futures market arbitrage plays in providing liquidity in their market, and to facilitate arbitrage there has always been a special Class B category of membership. The Class B member specialises in arbitrage between the IMM

and the forward market, and is exempt from margin requirements. An arrangement exists whereby the clearing house
guarantees the credit of Class B members with the banks; thus
the average Class B member who is small by interbank
standards can obtain keen terms in the forward exchange
market and the liquidity of the IMM is enhanced. A Class B
membership is obtained by applying to the clearing house and
satisfying it of one's creditworthiness. No payment is made.
Normally only a clearing member would be able to satisfy the
rigorous requirements of a successful application. A Class B
membership specifies only one bank with which the arbitrageur can conduct business free of margin requirement. The
clearing house informs the bank at the close of each business
day what open positions the Class B member has in currency
futures, thus enabling the bank to confirm that all deals with
itself have been offset exactly on the IMM. An individual
arbitrageur can obtain several Class B memberships.

In the early days of the IMM's existence, when overall
business volume in currency futures was much lower than
today, arbitrage operations occurred less flexibly. Because
trading volume on the IMM was low, banks would rarely find
that when they phoned up Class B members and informed
them of their current quote that any business would result.
Banks could not justify the costs of frequent communication
with the IMM given the infrequency of business arising
therefrom. A Class B member had to take the initiative of
communicating with banks and asking for quotes if he
suspected that a speculative run or large order on the floor
had led to a misalignment of quotes between the IMM and
forward market. The scope to match interbank and futures
quotes profitably at low risk (i.e. very close together in time)
was more circumscribed than under later conditions when
business was sufficiently active to justify banks (and bank
brokers) making continuous offers to the arbitrageur. In the
well-developed futures market of today the IMM arbitrageur
is usually aware of quotes that have recently been indicated to
him by banks, some of which indeed may hold good until
further notice for execution; thus having concluded a deal on
the floor the IMM arbitrageur can immediately confirm the
offsetting deal with a bank. It pays some banks to have

someone in their dealing room whose specific duty is communication with the IMM, and who shows at frequent intervals the bank's current quotes to the IMM arbitrageur with whom it has a relationship; sometimes the bank will make the IMM arbitrageur a one-way offer, in similar fashion to making an offer through an interbank broker. This latter technique is often used where the bank has excess inventory to clear. If the arbitrageur himself had to initiate all communication with banks, as in the early days of the IMM, he would only rarely hit by chance those banks with particularly imbalanced inventory and whose quotes would often be attractive for an arbitrage operation; but now that the IMM is a deep market, those banks would present their quotes on their own initiative to the IMM, hoping to dispose of inventory there. In sum, the IMM has developed from being a satellite of the forward market to being its associate; rather than dealers in the IMM initiating all communication with the forward market dealers, the relationship is now two-way.[9]

It may appear at first sight surprising that banks have not entered (with one or two exceptions) the arbitrage business between the IMM and the forward market as active participants, by buying a Class B membership themselves. Surely a bank which is active in the forward market should be able to execute arbitrage transactions at a lower cost than an IMM local? In particular, a bank which is a market-maker in the forward market may be able to offset an IMM deal with a transaction in the forward market at a keener rate than can a local arbitrageur. For example, suppose the bank is quoting DM/$ 2.3545–55 in the forward market, whilst market-makers on the IMM floor are quoting a $/DM rate equivalent to DM/$ 2.3549–59. Then a large buy order for dollars (say for $10m equivalent value) is presented on the IMM floor; the bank could offer to sell dollars at say 2.3560 (assuming that market-makers on the IMM have reduced their $/DM quotes) and simultaneously raise its DM/$ forward quote to say DM/$ 2.3546–56, hoping thereby to attract extra dollar sellers and detract dollar buyers in the forward market and so match the dollar sale which it has made on the IMM. On the extra foreign exchange turnover which the bank gains from this strategy, the bank earns additional revenue at the rate of the combined spread (14 pips – i.e. 2.3560 minus 2.3546); this type of additional revenue could not be realised by the IMM local. Suppose the arbitrage transaction in $10 million gives rise to a net increase in overall turnover for the bank of $5 million (the difference between gross and net increase in turnover is due to the change in the bank's forward quote causing some loss of buy orders for dollars). On the $ 5 million portion of the arbitrage business which represents a substitution instead of a net addition to foreign exchange turnover, the apparent rate of arbitrage profit can be less than for the IMM local because the bank must treat as an offset to profit raising its bid rate for dollars in the forward market in order to induce the profitable extra flow. Even so, taking the two portions of the arbitrage turnover together, the bank should be able to realise a larger profit than the local in the given example.

So far we have been comparing arbitrage by an IMM local between a given bank, say bank A, and the IMM floor, with arbitrage by bank A itself between the forward market and the IMM floor. In reality, the local does not need to confine his arbitrage to bank A; he is likely to be receiving and asking for quotes continuously from say banks B, C, and D (on the assumption that he has several Class B memberships). In the previous example, suppose that bank B's forward market quote just prior to the presentation of the large dollar buy order on the floor of the IMM was DM/$ 2.3541–51. This would probably indicate that compared to bank A, bank B had an excess long position in dollar inventory and an excess short position in mark inventory (with bank A having an excess long position in marks). The IMM local arbitrageur, in noticing the presentation of the large dollar buy order on the floor, would intend to match a sale of dollars at DM/$ 2.3560 on the floor not by buying dollars from bank A but rather from bank B. The potential profit from the local buying dollars from B at DM/$ 2.3551 and selling on the IMM at DM/$ 2.3560 may well be greater than the total *extra* profit which bank A can realise from performing the arbitrage transaction described earlier. Clearly bank B could make an even larger profit than the local in the above circumstances; but in other circumstances, often A's and B's quotes will be related to each other in a way such that B can make the larger arbitrage profit. If A and B each had a Class B membership of the IMM and had their own arbitrageur on the floor, only one would be active at any time, and the amount of arbitrage profit each made would possibly be insufficient to cover the expenses and capital costs of membership. A local, on the other hand, who could combine the business which A and B would effect, by dealing with whichever of the two would have been more favourably placed to conduct the particular piece of arbitrage business on its own account, could be active continuously and bear less fixed costs per unit of turnover.

The reader may question why in the above example, where A's and B's DM/$ quotes are 2.3546–56 and 2.3541–51 respectively, and where A but not B were a Class B member of the IMM, bank A itself does not simply bid dollars from B at DM/$ 2.3551 and sell them on the floor at DM/$ 2.356; equivalently, surely bank A could operate as a local would on the IMM floor, plus having the periodic advantage of being able to make larger arbitrage profit than the local, when A's quotes relative to other banks' made it worthwhile for A to adjust its quotes in the forward market and induce extra business turnover. Yet A would encounter difficulties in operating in this way. For sometimes the IMM arbitrageur does not have offers from the forward market to hand and must seek these; but A cannot simultaneously have a publicised quote in the interbank market of DM/$ 2.3546–56 and actively bid for dollars at a DM/$ rate above 2.3546 because it is aware of an arbitrage opportunity with the IMM. By acting in this way A's arbitrage team (the representative on the floor plus back-up at the head office dealing room) would pre-empt anyone offering dollars to head office at head office's bid rate, thus causing it to run an excess inventory position in marks possibly over a prolonged time-period. Even if A's arbitrage team does not make bids from other banks and asks simply for quotes, being ready to deal at above head office's quoted bid rate, this may undermine head office's attempts to dispose of excess mark inventory. For head office may have informed interbank brokers of the rate at which it is offering marks, and some banks may be confronted with an offer from a broker on A's behalf at one rate and from A's arbitrage team direct at another rate.

Although arbitrage plays an essential role in the maintenance of liquidity in the currency futures market, a very high ratio of arbitrage to 'indigenous' business would be a symptom of a weak market structure. A high ratio would imply that indigenous business had to bear the significant transaction cost of a high volume of offsetting business with the forward market. One advantage of the currency futures market, presented in the previous section, was that its form of organisation permits an economy to be made in interdealer activity; but this advantage would be reduced if the generation of liquidity in the futures market required a high volume of arbitrage business with the forward market to be effected. Under two types of conditions the proportion of arbitrage to indigenous business is likely to be high, and thereby the potential benefits of futures trading reduced: first, when trading volume in the futures market is low, implying that even moderate size orders cause price swings sufficient to make arbitrage business profitable; secondly, when speculative opinion in the futures market has become divergent from that in the forward market, so that speculative appetites in the IMM are satisfied by arbitrage transactions with the forward market, rather than by indigenous speculators dealing with each other. In practice, arbitrage business often has as its source a change of speculative opinion in the IMM not accompanied by a similar change in the forward market; the consensus view of IMM traders, dominated by short-term horizons and analysis of currency charts, often appears to differ from that of participants in the traditional exchange markets.

HEDGING IN CURRENCY FUTURES MARKETS

A principal advantage of commodity futures markets to the macro-economy is their provision of insurance services; producers and consumers can insure themselves against untoward movements in the commodity price. Facilities for hedging currency risks existed, of course, long before the innovation of currency futures markets; those at risk could insure themselves in the forward markets or by mismatching the currency denomination of their liabilities and assets. The subject of hedging currency risks has been treated widely in the economics literature.[10] The intention here is only to pinpoint various unresolved or non-highlighted issues.

Let us first consider the question of how the individual investor should measure his exposure to exchange risk. As an illustration, take a Swiss investor who is seeking to identify the currency composition of the monetary portfolio (in which instruments have a maturity of say, six months or less) for which the risk of returns would be least. The basket of currencies which is identified would be taken as the neutral portfolio relative to which the investor would measure risk. In choosing the weights for each currency in the basket, the Swiss should be influenced by three principal considerations – volatility of the *ex ante* real interest rate, real exchange rate risk, and inflation risk. The importance of each type of risk depends on how far ahead in time is the horizon up to which the investor is measuring returns from the portfolio.

Suppose our investor has a medium-term horizon, say four years into the future; his minimum risk monetary portfolio is that combination of international monies (invested in instruments with maximum maturity of three months) for which the probability distribution of real returns (measured over the four years ahead) has lowest variance. To calculate the overall real return from the portfolio, nominal returns (measured in francs) are deflated by an index of the franc price of goods which our investor buys. In order to cumulate prospective real returns over the next four years, the investor must make an assumption about the *ex ante* real short-term rate of interest that will prevail on roll-over dates for each currency brand of monetary instrument. In his estimation of the variance of the cumulative real return from the portfolio, he should acknowledge that the *ex ante* real rate of interest on any money (measured relative to inflation in the country of issue) at a given roll-over date is not independent of its rate at the previous roll-over date. If the *ex ante* real rate jumps above its historical average during this period, it is also likely to be above its historical average next period. In more technical language, the probability distribution, from which the expected real return on a money in each period is drawn, is neither constant nor random through time.

The probability distributions, from which the short-term (*ex ante*) real rates of interest on each money (measured relative to expected inflation in each respective issuing country) for any period are drawn, are somewhat interdependent, but not completely so. Thus the investor, by diversifying his monetary portfolio, should be able to reduce the variance of the probability distribution from which its overall real return (measured over the four-year period) will be drawn. The further ahead in time is the investor's horizon, the more important does real interest rate volatility (measured relative to inflation in each respective issuing country) and the less important does real exchange rate volatility become as an explanation of variability of overall real return from the portfolio. For cumulative real exchange rate movement over time is limited by the pull of the anchor of purchasing power parity whilst cumulative real interest rate differentials are in principle unlimited.

The increasing importance of real interest-rate volatility and decreasing importance of real exchange-rate volatility in explaining the variance of the overall real return from the portfolio, as the horizon is extended, suggests that long-term investors should diversify more across the boundary of their currency zone than do short-term investors.[11] For the probability distribution, from which the *ex ante* real return on a money-market instrument denominated in a dollar zone currency is drawn, is more independent of that for an instrument in a mark zone currency (e.g. Swiss francs, Deutsche marks) than of that for an instrument in another dollar zone currency; and the importance of exchange rate risk, which is greater for trans-zonal than intra-zonal exchange rates, decreases as the horizon is pushed forward in time. It is assumed that inflation risk, the source of difference between the *ex ante* and *ex post* real interest rate, is of similarly small magnitude for short-term instruments (up to six months' maturity) in the major international monies. The greater interdependence of intra-zonal *ex ante* real interest rates (and thereby usually of *ex post* real interest rates, except where inflation risk is considerable for at least one of the monetary instruments being compared) than of trans-zonal real interest rates is due to the normally strong economic interdependence of countries lying in the same currency zone and their limited scope for pursuing independent monetary policies.[12]

The second consideration relevant to determining the optimum extent of international diversification is exchange risk. The Swiss investor's consumption is likely to be spread between goods and services coming from many countries. Thus a large proportion of the goods and services which he purchases are highly sensitive in price to the behaviour of the Swiss franc in the foreign exchange market. These internationally traded goods (goods whose price is exchange-rate sensitive – usually imports or close import substitutes) fall into two main categories – DM-goods and $-goods. The franc price of DM-goods is most sensitive to the franc/mark rate (DM-goods are usually produced and consumed predominantly within Europe); similarly the franc price of dollar-goods is most sensitive to the franc/dollar rate.

Suppose that the Swiss National Bank is pursuing a long-term policy of holding inflation in Switzerland to around 3% per annum, allowing some overshoot in years when the franc, measured against its effective index, is weak, whilst ensuring that some undershoot occurs in years when the franc is strong. Under this policy, fluctuations in the franc price of the investor's shopping basket, when measured over short periods of time, say one year or less, would be highly sensitive to the franc's exchange rate, particularly the franc/mark rate, given the likely high proportion of DM-goods therein. If the investor's time-horizon were close to the present, a portfolio weighted substantially towards the Deutsche mark should prove to be of lower risk than one invested entirely in Swiss francs. However, were the investor's horizon further into the future, the international spread of his consumption would provide less justification for monetary diversification; for real interest rates on francs would tend to rise in the aftermath of a significant depreciation of the franc's effective index, as the Swiss National Bank acted to slow inflation back to its long-run path. The high real income on francs during this subsequent period of disinflation, which may extend over a period of years, should often compensate the investor for the real loss on francs caused by the initial inflation shock.

Were the Swiss investor's pattern of expenditure atypical (for a Swiss) – for example, with a heavy concentration on $-goods – or were he unsure about his expenditure pattern beyond the short-run (for example, he may not be sure whether he will still be resident in Switzerland), he would not be impressed greatly by the suggestion that periods of high real interest rates on francs should tend to compensate him for unexpected inflation in Switzerland (caused by a bout of weakness in the franc's effective index). The inflation rate, measured as the rate of increase in the franc price of his shopping basket, would be more sensitive to the dollar/franc rate than would be the inflation rate measured by the Swiss consumer price index. An appreciation of the dollar, which may have little impact on the franc's effective index and Swiss inflation rate, and so not cause a rise in franc interest rates, would bring about a rise in the franc price of this particular Swiss's shopping basket.

In the above example, real exchange rate risk was the assumed source of inflation variability. But were home-grown inflation also highly variable, then the investor could obtain a reduction in portfolio risk through international diversification even were his consumption concentrated almost entirely on domestic goods. For instance, if home-grown inflation (i.e. that part of inflation which can not be attributed to real exchange rate fluctuation) in Switzerland varied (at an annual rate) with a standard deviation of 15% in each three-month period, then the risk of real returns from the monetary portfolio could be reduced substantially by diversification into foreign monies, particularly those of low real interest rate volatility (and thereby of low inflation risk). The further ahead is the investor's horizon, the more important is the risk of home-grown inflation as a factor favouring international diversification. For real exchange-rate movement is limited by the anchor of purchasing power parity, whilst cumulative error of the money markets in estimating inflation (and this error is an important source of *ex post* real interest-rate volatility) is unlimited over time.

Inflation risk as a factor promoting currency diversification is a special case of the more general factor of *ex post* real interest-rate volatility. Volatility of the *ex post* real interest rate, measured over say three-month periods, has two sources; first, volatility of the *ex ante* real interest rate and second, unexpected change in the inflation rate. The *ex ante* real interest rate is not constant through time, and as explained earlier, its level in one period is not independent of its level in previous periods; this interdependence increases the variance of the probability distribution from which multi-period real returns are drawn. If the market is efficient in its formation of inflation expectations, error in estimating inflation in one period should be independent of error in previous periods; cumulative inflation error still climbs with distance to the horizon, but at a declining rate (provided that the variance of the probability distribution from which inflation is drawn in each period does not increase with time).

So far we have been considering exchange risk from the viewpoint of the individual investor. He faces a risk-return trade-off. By distorting currency proportions away from those in his minimum risk portfolio, he can often increase his expected rate of return. Which point he chooses on the efficient frontier of monetary portfolios (constructed to fit his time-horizon and spending pattern) depends on his degree of risk-aversion. The hedging decision of the corporation – how much exchange risk to accept and defined in terms of which numeraire – is usually quite different from the hedging decision of the individual investor. By setting a maximum limit to the amount of exchange risk exposure, the corporation assures its creditors (bond holders and banks) that it will not gamble on the exchange market; without such an assurance, creditors would charge a hefty risk premium to protect themselves against the corporation increasing its exchange risk exposure and incurring large losses. As long as shareholders know the numeraire against which the corporation is controlling risk, and are confident that this risk can be limited strictly, they are not impeded in balancing their portfolio between different currencies in desired fixed proportions. It is not of great importance to the shareholders what numeraire is chosen, so long as it is publicly known. If, in contrast, the numeraire were unknown, then the shareholder would be uncertain about how his portfolio was divided between different currency risks.

The private corporation, like the public corporation, normally sets a limit to the exchange risk which it will assume. It does so first to assure its creditors and second to limit the risk borne by its own shareholders who do not have great scope (unlike shareholders in a large public corporation) to diversify away risks assumed in the corporation. The choice of numeraire against which risk is measured is of great importance to the shareholders, given the large share of their portfolio which equity in the private corporation represents. For example, a private UK company whose shareholders concentrate their expenditures in Switzerland, would adopt a numeraire which was heavily weighted towards the franc.

A hedging problem often faced by a corporation is whether or not to buy foreign currency forward to meet payment against invoices several weeks from now. For example, consider a British retail company which is stocking up German electrical goods in anticipation of the busy Christmas season, and which finds that most of the invoices (denominated in marks) fall due for payment at end-September, having placed the orders in the summer months. The price (in pounds) at which these electrical goods can be sold will be influenced by the average mark/pound rate over the August to October period; for competitor retailers in aggregate buy their marks over a range of dates, spanning August to October, and the average cost of the electrical goods to the retail trade will be most sensitive to the average mark/pound rate. It is the average cost which is assumed to be relevant to the setting of retail prices. To hedge exchange risk, the retail company must try to buy marks at the average August/October rate. It does this by dividing its total marks bill into twelve equal parts, spreading the part purchase over twelve weeks. At end-September, the corporation's treasurer meets due payment by applying marks bought to date plus buying the balance in the spot market; simultaneously the treasurer would sell this same balance of marks forward for delivery at end-October. In each subsequent week, the treasurer continues to buy marks (according to the original schedule) and applies these eventually to the closing out of his mark forward contract at end-October.

In the above example, it has been assumed implicitly that there are no close substitutes for the German goods that can be purchased both in Britain and elsewhere. However, competitor retailers may have contracted to purchase electrical goods from British manufacturers, and should the Deutsche mark rise strongly from June to October, our retailer may not be able to maintain his customary profit margin. In these circumstances, retailers would tend to buy marks forward around the time of placing orders with German suppliers. The average forward price of the mark during June to August, the period in which orders are placed, would then be the most relevant exchange-rate variable to the determination of electrical goods' retail price. The retailer who placed most of his orders in June, could hedge exchange risk best by spreading his purchases of mark forward contracts (for October delivery) over the June to August period. In addition, the retailer should take out some extra mark forward cover in June, with maturity in August, to cover himself against the risk that the mark may rise strongly over the order-placing period, whereby those competitor retailers who placed orders late on could scale back their purchases of German goods and increase their domestic purchases, so putting our retailer at a competitive disadvantage.[13] Conceptually the retailer should identify the exchange-rate variable to which his profit is most closely sensitive; this is likely to be a weighted average of the forward exchange rates quoted during the payment period. The zero-risk hedging strategy would then involve staggered purchases both in the spot and forward exchange markets.

NOTES

1. See P. Einzig, *A Dynamic Theory of Forward Exchange* (London: Macmillan, 1975) ch. 1.
2. Time-stamping is a precaution against dishonesty, as it allows exchange officials to check the history of how each order was fulfilled.

3. See J. M. Burns, 'Electronic Trading in Futures Markets', *Financial Analysts Journal* (February 1982) for a description of this particular type of abuse.
4. All contract specifications here are based on practices in 1982.
5. In the swap market, simultaneous spot and forward transactions are effected. When a customer swaps marks into dollars for three months, he sells spot marks for dollars, and simultaneously sells the dollars forward for marks three months forward. An active market exists in swap exchange deals.
6. A swap transaction can be shown to be equivalent to a borrow and lend operation; see B. D. Brown, 'The Swap Market and its Relation to Currency Forward and Futures Markets', in *Futures Markets*, ed. M. E. Streit (Oxford: Blackwell, 1983).
7. His choice between the two strategies will depend on the degree of inflation uncertainty (high inflation uncertainty would make him favour the roll-over strategy) and of correlation between the swap rate and immediate past movement of the spot rate (a high correlation would make him favour a long-term forward contract).
8. The liquidity of the June contract would begin to diminish somewhat from end-April onwards, as the September contract would begin to take over from the April contract as the centre of trading attention.
9. See B. D. Brown, *Money Hard and Soft* (London: Macmillan, 1978) ch. 1, for an elaboration of this distinction.
10. For a treatment of currency-risk hedging, see R. Z. Aliber, *Exchange Risk and Corporate International Finance* (London: Macmillan, 1978).
11. Currencies which move closely together in the exchange markets form a 'currency zone' (e.g. the US and Canadian dollars). An investor makes a trans-zonal investment if he placed funds in a currency that does not belong to the same zone as his numeraire currency.
12. Because exchange risk of intra-zonal exchange rates is less than that of trans-zonal rates, capital flows are more sensitive to intra- than to trans-zonal interest rate differentials. Thus, for example, the effective index of the Dutch guilder should prove more sensitive to the guilder/mark than to the dollar/guilder interest-rate differential. If the Dutch central bank has one aim of policy the limiting of fluctuations in the effective index of the

guilder, Dutch interest rates should be more dependent on German than on US rates.

13. As a corollary, the retailer who places his orders domestically in June, should sell marks forward for August to cover himself against the risk that the mark will fall, and competitors who place their orders later could buy cheaper German goods.

3 Short-term Interest-rate Futures

Interest-rate futures markets represent a greater break from the past than do currency futures markets. Until T-bill futures were launched on the IMM in the mid-1970s, it had not been possible for the general public to deal in dollar money-market instruments for forward delivery. In contrast, currency futures markets had been born into a world in which an already liquid market in currency forwards existed. The short-term interest-rate futures contracts differ in an important respect from other futures. In all other futures contracts, the commodity can be bought in the spot market at any time during the contract's lifetime. Consider, however, a 91-day T-bill futures contract maturing on 15 June. A 91-day T-bill running from 15 June has a butterfly existence; it is issued on 15 June and by the next day it has become a 90-day bill. The spot market for T-bills with 91 days to maturity starting from 15 June is open for only one day. The butterfly existence of the commodity underlying the short-term interest-rate futures contract causes market-making and speculation in interest-rate futures to differ in important respects from those in other futures markets.

Just as currency futures business received a boost from the breakdown of fixed exchange rates in 1973, business in interest-rate futures gained from the floating of short-term dollar interest rates in 1979. At that time, the Federal Reserve ceased to peg over short period of time its key intervention rate in the overnight money market. The resulting increase in volatility of interest rates caused a wide range

69

of speculators and hedgers to enter the interest-rate futures markets. Unlike for currency futures, no active forward market coexists alongside interest rate futures. Thus the latter represent a radical departure in trading possibilities for both small and large corporations. Like for currencies, the most active markets in interest-rate futures are now found in Chicago. Small, less active markets exist also in London, Toronto, and Sydney.

THE CONTRACTS

By far the most popular short-term interest-rate futures contract has been that for 91-day US T-bills. Other contracts have included those for short-term commercial paper, short-term euro-dollar deposits and domestic US certificates of deposits. T-bill futures are traded only on Chicago's IMM; CD futures have been traded on the IMM, on Chicago's Board of Trade, and the New York Futures Exchange; commercial paper has been traded on the Board of Trade; euro-dollar deposit futures have been traded both on the Chicago IMM and on the London International Financial Futures Exchange (LIFFE).

The design of T-bill futures contracts is simple. Each contract is for a three-month US Treasury bill having a face value at maturity of $1 000 000. Prices are quoted in terms of the IMM index. (For example, a T-bill yield of 7.50 would be quoted as 92.50. In the cash market for T-bills, yields are quoted on a discount basis; the yield quoted is the difference between the face value of a bill and its market value on an annualised basis.) Futures contracts are traded for four delivery months – March, June, September and December. Futures trading for a particular maturity (e.g. March) terminates on the second business day following the Federal Reserve three-month T-bill auction. Delivery must be made on the business day following the last day of trading; delivery is made to a Chicago bank, registered with the IMM and a member of the Federal Reserve System, specified by the buyer's clearing member (physical delivery rarely occurs; instead offsetting entries are made to T-bill accounts which member banks maintain with the Federal Reserve). At the seller's option, a delivery unit may be composed of US Treasury bills bearing maturities of 91 or 92 days. All bills in a delivery unity must bear uniform maturity dates.

The essentials of trading T-bill futures are similar to those of currency futures. Trading, however, is somewhat less concentrated on the nearest delivery month than it is for currencies. In part this is due to a greater proportion of business in T-bill futures than in currency futures being carried out by hedgers (for there is no parallel bank market in which hedgers can deal on a forward basis). Also the futures prices for different delivery months are less closely correlated for T-bill futures than for currency futures, and so the hedger on the T-bill futures market, as opposed to the currency futures market, is unlikely to favour mismatching the maturity of his hedge in order to deal in the most liquid delivery month (the nearest). The possibility of inter-temporal arbitrage is responsible for the high correlation of currency futures prices across delivery months. Buying pressure on the June Deutsche mark contract would stimulate arbitrageurs to buy the March Deutsche mark contract and swap the marks into dollars for three months under a forward swap contract with June delivery. Thus upward pressure would be transmitted to the March contract. In contrast, if buying pressure develops for the June T-bill contract, no arbitrage opportunity is created which involves the March T-bill contract; indeed a T-bill bought in March would have 'melted' into cash by June.

Managing inventory positions in different delivery months of the same commodity is somewhat more complicated for T-bill futures (and other short-term money-market instruments) than for other commodity (including currency) futures. Some independent floor traders concentrate on dealing in spreads between different delivery months. For example, in the gold pit, a spread trader on noticing buying pressure on the June contract not matched on the March contract may sell June gold and buy March gold. Given that business volume is higher in the nearer delivery month, the readiness of the spread trader to assume intra-delivery month exposure is essential to the creation of liquidity in the back months (further distant delivery months). The spread trader in gold can, moreover, reduce his risk exposure by offsetting contracts in T-bill futures (see section on arbitrage below); he can match his long position in March gold and short position in June gold by taking a short position in a March T-bill. The spread-trader in gold does not have to liquidate his position in the two delivery months before maturity by effecting a new transaction on the floor. He can simply take delivery of gold under the March contract, borrow to finance the holding of gold inventory until June, and deliver the gold under the June contract.

Consider next how the spread-trader operates in the T-bill futures market. Suppose, like in the gold example, he notices that there is buying pressure for June T-bills unmatched by buying pressure for March T-bills. Again the spread trader may take simultaneously a short position in the June contract and a long position in the March contract, anticipating that the price difference between the two contracts will narrow. But the price of different delivery months are less highly correlated for T-bill futures than for gold (or currencies), and so the spread trader in T-bills is assuming more risk in operating as a scalper in response to a bunching of orders in one delivery month than his counterpart in the gold or currency pits. The spreader in T-bill futures must liquidate his position in the two delivery months prior to maturity; he cannot engage in a 'cash and carry' operation like the gold spreader. If he took delivery of a March T-bill, and maintained his position in the June contract, he would run an open position in June T-bills for three months, which is far from being a zero-risk position. The 91-day T-bill delivered in March would have matured into cash by June, and the spot sale of the June T-bill would have been completely uncovered. Thus the spread trader described would intend to close out both positions before the expiry of the March contract.

The design of short-term money-market instrument contracts other than T-bills has been complicated by illiquidity of the spot markets and by non-standardisation of the commodity to be delivered. For instance, consider the design of a bank CD futures contract. CDs are not issued according to a regular calendar (unlike T-bills) even by the largest banks.

There may be very few CDs maturing within a narrow span of time that may be bought either in the secondary or primary markets. The designers of the CD contract have tried to overcome the potential problem of illiquidity in the cash market by allowing flexibility in the maturity delivery date and in the name of the CD contract that may be delivered. On the IMM the person with a short position in a CD futures contract can choose any day to deliver in the period beginning on the 15th day of the delivery month, and ending on the last business day of the delivery month. The CD delivered must not have a maturity before the 16th of the month three months after the spot month and not after the last day of the month three months after the spot month. The seller can deliver CDs from a list of eligible bank names determined periodically by the IMM. On the second business day preceding the 15th calendar day of each month, the IMM staff updates a list of domestic certificates of deposit that are considered by the cash market to be of the highest liquidity, lowest credit risk, and which trade at identical yields. The list is formed by selecting a random sample of at least seven dealers from a list of at least ten dealers who actively participate in the domestic CD market. The bank names that are common to at least five lists in the sample and have agreed to be deliverable on the contract comprise the list of deliverable CD issues.

By permitting the seller to deliver one out of several CD names, the risk of a squeeze on the cash market is reduced. A squeeze would arise where the accumulated long positions requiring delivery exceeded the total supply of deliverable CDs. In that situation the longs could extract large sums from the shorts, in compensation for non-fulfilment of contract. A long trader may himself foster a squeeze by buying up CDs in the cash market ahead of the delivery period, thus hoping to create a shortage of deliverable CDs; as shorts pushed up the price of the particular name of CD as they attempted to meet their delivery obligation, the long trader may supply some CDs out of his accumulated inventory at an inflated price. IMM rules are designed to prevent such manipulation, and any long trader is allowed to accumulate positions only up to a limited extent.

Allowing shorts to deliver one of several names reduces the risk of manipulation, but it introduces a new potential, albeit soluble, problem. The problem relates to a change in the relative credit rankings of CDs. For example, if the IMM specified a range of bank names that could be delivered when a delivery month was first listed, and one of those names (say bank A) fell in status during the lifetime of the existing contract, then shorts would decide to deliver bank A CDs on maturity, because they could be bought relatively cheaply in the cash market. Indeed, as soon as bank A fell in status, the price of futures contracts would fall to reflect the expectation that it would be a secondary rather than a prime name CD that would be delivered against the futures contract. It was to avoid such delivery and price uncertainty that the IMM decided against specifying an unchanged list of deliverable CDs during the lifetime of each contract. Instead, the list of deliverable CDs is updated monthly and it is not until two days before the start of the delivery period for any particular contract that the list of CD names that are deliverable is known with certainty.

The flexibility of delivery date and of length to maturity (of the delivered CD) which the CD futures contract permits are themselves relevant to the setting of the futures price and complicate the relation between the futures price and the expected spot price of CDs on maturity. Consider first the contract from the viewpoint of the person with the short position, Mr Short. If at the start of the delivery period, say at mid-June, the yield curve in the CD market is very steep, then Mr Short can gain from delivering immediately a CD with a maturity of end-September rather than waiting to effect delivery at the end of the month, when the maximum maturity of the CD deliverable is three months rather than $3\frac{1}{2}$ months.[1] In contrast if the yield curve in the CD market is downward sloping, then Mr Short can gain from waiting to carry out delivery until the end of June, and then delivering a CD which matures on 18 September, the shortest maturity CD which is deliverable. The person with a long position in the CD futures contract, Mr Long, is aware of course that Mr Short can gain from the flexibility provided by the contract. Consequently the maximum price at which he would buy CD futures, say for

June, would show an equivalent interest rate somewhat higher than what he expects three-month CD yields will be in June.[2] In effect, Mr Long requires a premium to protect himself against the yield curve becoming steep in either an upward or downward direction, and to allow for any steepness in the present yield curve at the time of entering into the contract. Even though Mr Short can effect delivery from mid-June onwards, trading of June CDs continues up to the end of the month. If the yield curve is already downward sloping at mid-June, then Mr Short faces the possibility of making additional profit until end-June should the degree of downward sloping increase.[3]

In the late 1970s, the Chicago Board of Trade (CBT) experimented with another type of short-term interest-rate contract – that for commercial paper. But the contract did not prove successful. There is not an active secondary market in commercial paper, and so the cash-futures arbitrage transactions that are generally important to futures market liquidity were not possible. The contract was designed so that the list of eligible paper for delivery was specified when contracts for a given delivery month started trading. Thus the futures price was sensitive to any divergence that opened up between the market appraisal of the eligible names during the lifetime of a contract.

In late 1981, the IMM introduced a new form of short-term interest-rate contract that was designed to avoid the complications of variable delivery dates, maturities and names. The new three-month euro-dollar futures contract did not provide for the physical delivery of any security on maturity; instead the contract was based on the principle of cash settlement. Any non-liquidated positions remaining at the clearing house on the last day of trading (two days before maturity of the contract) are closed out by cash settlement. The IMM determines a final settlement price as the average offer price for three-month euro-dollar deposits in the London interbank market (LIBOR).

The average is determined in a way to minimise the risk of error or of false reporting. The clearing house determines the LIBOR rate both at the time of termination of trading (3.30 p.m. London time) and at a randomly selected time within the last 90 minutes of trading. At either time, the clearing house selects at random 12 reference banks from a list of no less than 20 participating banks that are major banks in the London euro-$ market. Each reference bank quotes to the clearing house its perception of the rate at which three-month euro-dollar time deposit funds are currently offered by the market to prime banks. The two highest and lowest quotes are omitted in calculation of the average.

Profits (or losses) on open contracts at the close of trading are calculated as the difference between the closing price of the day before and the final settlement price and are paid out to (or received from) clearing members on their outstanding position. The London International Financial Futures Exchange (LIFFE) has adopted a similar system of cash settlements with respect to its futures contracts. The euro-$ CD cash market is not as liquid as the domestic US CD cash market, and so a euro-$ futures contract which called for physical delivery would be seriously subject to risk of manipulation and squeezes.

Until the introduction of cash settlement with respect to the euro-dollar contract and soon after with respect to the stock index futures (see Chapter 6), US futures exchanges had always insisted that physical delivery be provided for under all contracts. Cash settlement is a feasible alternative only where there is a clear reference price that is produced in the cash market and which is itself not subject to manipulation. It would be possible for one of the reference banks to quote an artificially high euro-dollar rate to the IMM and hope to profit thereby from a below average settlement price (assuming the particular reference bank had a short position in the euro-dollar contract). But the scope for profit by such manipulation is small, given the complex procedure already described by which the IMM calculates the final settlement price.

ARBITRAGE BETWEEN INTEREST-RATE FUTURES AND CASH MARKETS

We saw in the previous chapter that arbitrage between the traditional forward exchange market and the currency futures market played an important role in making the latter liquid. Similarly in the interest-rate futures markets, the possibility of arbitrage with parallel conventional markets is essential to the creation of liquidity. Let us take first the example of the T-bill futures market.

Suppose today's date is 24 April. A trader could offset completely the risk of a short position in a June T-bill futures contract (for which the delivery date is, say, 24 June), by buying in the cash market a five-month T-bill, and simultaneously entering into a sale-and-repurchase transaction, whereby he sells the five-month T-bill spot and agrees to repurchase the T-bill on 24 June (when it will have shrunk to being a three-month bill): the cash derived from the sale-and-repurchase agreement finances the spot purchase of the bill. There is a very active sale-and-repurchase market for T-bills and US Government bonds in New York, with the principal participants being securities dealers, investment institutions and banks.

In effect, a sale-and-repurchase agreement is a form of secured borrowing; the lender is the party which buys the bill and agrees to re-sell it to the other party at a fixed price (the resale price is agreed at the same time as the purchase price). An institution which is in temporary need of extra cash can engage simply in a sale-and-repurchase agreement rather than incurring transaction costs of selling and re-buying. The interest rates set under sale-and-repurchase agreements (calculated from the premium of the agreed repurchase rate over the spot rate) are usually somewhat lower than that on equivalent maturity transactions in Federal funds, due to the secured nature of the former. Yet the sale-and-repurchase rate is usually somewhat higher than a simple T-bill rate (calculated on identical yield basis) for the same maturity. Thus the implicit forward rate for 91-day T-bills for delivery on 24 June, calculated by comparing the yield on a five-month

T-bill with that on a two-month T-bill (as quoted on 24 April), can be very slightly above the June T-bill futures rate without there being a profitable arbitrage opportunity. The relevant rates to compare for the purpose of assessing arbitrage opportunity are the five-month T-bill rate, the T-bill futures rate, and the three-month sale-and-repurchase rate.

Arbitrage is also possible in the direction opposite to that just described. A trader can offset completely the risk of a long position in a June T-bill futures by entering into a two-month sale-and-repurchase agreement, buying a five-month T-bill spot and simultaneously selling it two months forward, and also selling the five-month T-bill (received under the sale-and-repurchase agreement) for cash; on 24 June he buys a three-month T-bill to meet his obligation under the sale-and-repurchase agreement. In the sale-and-repurchase market trading is usually on an unspecific basis. The party selling spot and re-buying forward does not specify at the time of dealing what exact maturity of security will be delivered. In recent years, however, a narrow market for sale-and-repurchase in specific issues has grown up, with the party obtaining the securities specifying the particular issue. Thus the arbitrageur described can specify that he wants a five-month T-bill to be delivered under the sale-and-repurchase agreement. The relative narrowness of the sale-and-repurchase market for specific issues causes profitable arbitrage opportunity in the direction of buying T-bill futures, and offsetting this in the sale-and-repurchase plus cash markets, rarer than arbitrage opportunity in the opposite direction.

Arbitrage between the T-bill futures market, the sale-and-repurchase market, and the cash T-bill market is a special example of a general set of triangular arbitrage operations. In contrast, arbitrage operations between the currency futures and forward markets are linear rather than triangular, involving operations in two markets only. As with the currency futures example, arbitrage transactions between the T-bill futures and sale-and-repurchase markets are generally effected by IMM locals rather than by dealers in other markets. A local trader on the floor would respond to a big buy order presented for T-bill futures by outbidding the scalpers and offsetting his resulting exposure by dealing in the spot T-bill and the sale-and-repurchase markets. As in the currency futures markets, dealers in the parallel conventional market (here the sale-and-repurchase market) and spot bill market are likely to approach IMM arbitrageurs when they are in inventory imbalance (with respect to their own market).

Unlike Treasury securities, a sale-and-repurchase market does not exist for CDs. In principle an IMM dealer could lay off exposure in CD futures by borrowing and lending for different maturities. For example, on 15 April he could offset a long exposure in June CD futures by borrowing for a five-month period (at a fixed interest rate) and lending simultaneously for a two-month period (also at a fixed rate). If he concluded both the borrowing and deposit transaction with the same bank, undertaking to repay the borrowing at two months on the basis of the then three-month interest rate, the margin which the bank would charge between borrowing and lending rates would not have to include a premium against the risk of default. But the dealer would be a captive client of the bank with which the transactions were arranged, having to accept its proposal on terms for repaying the loan after two months. In addition, banks do not usually quote deposit and loan rates for odd maturities and where one is requested by a customer the quotation is likely to be unfavourable.

Banks themselves are better placed than the IMM dealer to undertake arbitrage transactions between the interbank money markets and the CD futures market. In the course of taking on deposits and making loans, they are likely to incur substantial gaps in their money book. For example, in mid-March a bank may have made a large volume of six-month fixed-rate loans and covered this with customers' deposits which mature mostly in June. Originally, the bank may have had little concern about the exposure to interest-rate risk, believing moreover that interest rates would move so as to make the gap profitable, but by April, however, the bank has changed its view and wishes to close the gap. Before the advent of CD futures trading, the bank could have offset its resulting exposure to interest-rate risk only by borrowing longer term money and lending short term in the interbank market. It would probably have chosen to bid for six-month deposits and lend three-months, though not closing the gap entirely, in order to avoid dealing in illiquid non-standard maturities. But now the gap could be closed by the bank taking a short position in a June CD futures on the IMM. The strategy is attractive for the bank, as it can thereby reduce its interest-rate exposure without expanding its balance sheet and its loans in the interbank market. This consideration is of particular importance at times of crisis in the international banking system, when banks are trying to reduce their commitments to one another. The innovation of CD futures trading gives banks the opportunity to split the management of their exposure to interest-rate risk from that of maturity distribution (on both sides of the balance sheet).

Some banks take a more active role in arbitrage than simply calling up the IMM when a substantial gap develops in their money book. These banks monitor whether the CD futures rate is sufficiently out of alignment with the structure of money-market rates to make it profitable to expand their balance sheet by borrowing and lending in the interbank deposit market, offsetting these transactions by dealing in the CD futures markets. The intended offset is often not exact, with the bank choosing to deal in the more liquid standard maturity deposit markets. The bank can arbitrage more flexibly than the IMM dealer as it is a market-maker in the interbank deposit markets, and does not suffer from becoming a captive client of one particular bank. Arbitrage by banks keeps CD futures rates in line with implicit forward CD rates quoted.[4] The CD futures rate may be somewhat below the equivalent implicit forward rate, as the futures contract guarantees that only a top-class CD may be delivered, whilst a long-term CD (equivalent to a short-term CD plus a forward purchase of the same name of CD) bought in the cash market may deteriorate in quality over its lifetime. Sometimes, however, allowance for the seller's particular advantage in a CD futures contract may in fact bias CD futures rates in the opposite direction relative to implicit forward rates (see p.75).

It may strike the reader as strange that banks themselves have not made a market in forward CDs, which would be related to the CD futures markets in much the same way as the forward exchange market is related to the currency futures market. But the key ingredients of the CD futures contract that promote its liquidity – a range of deliverable names that is re-determined at monthly intervals, a flexible delivery date and a flexible maturity of the deliverable CD – could not have been incorporated in a direct forward market. Inter-dealer activity would have been complicated in a CD forward market; a bank which covered a net commitment to deliver its own CDs forward by buying CDs forward from other banks would be exposed to credit risk – that the quality of its own CDs may improve relative to those which it had purchased forward. A forward CD market would offer traders little protection against squeezes; for example, a bank may have contracted to buy a large number of its own CDs forward and then during the period when these contracts mature issue very few CDs in the cash market, so driving up their price and being able to obtain cheap finance. Buyers of a CD forward would take on the risk that the particular name designating the contract could deteriorate in credit quality over its lifetime.

When banks arbitrage with the CD futures market, they become a direct party to an IMM futures contract. This contrasts with arbitrage in the currency futures market where the bank writes a forward contract with the IMM Class B member who himself matches this with a currency futures contract. When the bank seeks to close a gap in its money book by dealing in the CD futures market it cannot obtain an instantaneous quote from the IMM; at best it can receive a report on the most recent prices obtained. The price which the bank will receive for a CD futures depends on the result of the particular auction when its order is announced to the floor by open outcry. Knowing the implicit rate at which the gap could be closed in the interbank market, the bank is likely to give a limit-order to its IMM broker with a fixed time allowed for fulfilment, where the price in the limit-order was somewhat more favourable than the implicit rate from the interbank market. In the much more volatile currency market, a bank would be loathe to leave a limit-order with an IMM dealer; the comparative quotes in the conventional interbank market could shift very rapidly, and the bank can find that it could have offset its exposure more cheaply than at the limit price achieved on the IMM.

OTHER ARBITRAGE TRANSACTIONS IN INTEREST-RATE FUTURES

Arbitrageurs are active not only between interest-rate futures and the money markets, but also between the interest-rate futures and commodity or currency futures markets. Let us take the example of arbitrage with the commodity futures markets first. Consider a merchant in copper who typically builds up inventory of copper during the second quarter of a year, as this is when customer demand is seasonally high. His merchanting income is derived from being able to supply immediately the needs of customers in his vicinity, and being able to deliver material in the shape and size requested. The merchant can hedge himself against the risk that the net running cost of holding hedged inventory[5] – during the period of inventory bulge starting in March – will be much larger than expected, by buying March and selling June copper futures at the same time as he commits himself to lease extra warehouse space for the second quarter, probably sometime during the previous autumn.

For example, in September the merchant may face futures prices for March and June the next year with the second month at a 12% *per annum* premium over the first; yet the merchant may expect storage and financing costs over the same interval to amount to 14% *per annum*. The merchant would intend to hold inventory up to that level so that marginal merchanting income is earned at the rate of 2% *per annum* (on inventory value). He would buy March and sell June futures to the physical extent of the anticipated bulge in inventory and arrange to rent the calculated amount of extra warehouse space. When March arrived, the merchant would intend to close out his position in the March contract while continuing to run the June position.

Though the merchant has reduced his risk exposure by dealing in the manner described, he has not eliminated it entirely. Two principal sources of risk remain. First, the level of the three-month interest rate in March may be very different from what the merchant expected it to be in that month. For example, the three-month interest rate in March may be 20% p.a. rather than the 13% p.a. expected. A large loss would then be incurred on merchanting activity. In line with the rise in interest rates, the premium of the June futures price over the now spot March price would have widened (although not necessarily by the same amount as the interest rate), and so a loss would be incurred if the merchant simply closed out all futures positions rather than taking delivery. The merchant can protect himself against this type of interest-rate risk by taking a short position in a CD futures (or T-bill futures) contract for March delivery. By combining the spread between March and June copper futures with a short position in a March interest-rate futures, the merchant hedges his income against both untoward changes in interest rates and in the convenience rent on copper.[6]

The second risk to which the merchant remains exposed, even after having entered into the interest-rate futures contract, is what has usually been described as basis risk. To illustrate this, imagine that when the merchant enters into the copper spread in September, the March and June futures prices are respectively 60 ¢s and 61.8 ¢s (per pound of material). By March the price of copper has shot up, whilst interest rates and the convenience rent have remained unchanged;[7] but suppose that in March the spot and June futures price had reached 100 ¢s and 103 ¢s respectively. The merchant would have made a 40 ¢ per pound profit on the March contract, and a 41.2 ¢ per pound loss on the June contract. Under the rules of futures exchanges, profits and losses must be cleared in cash daily, thus by March the merchant would have suffered a cash loss equivalent to 1.2 ¢s per pound. The requirement of daily cash settlement in futures markets is the essential cause of basis risk.

If, as in the London Metal Exchange – which is a forward market rather than a futures market – profit and loss is settled at maturity of the contract, basis risk would not exist. In the example, the merchant would receive 40 ¢ per pound in March, and would pay out 41.2 ¢s in June. He could invest the sum received in March in a three-month fixed term money-market instrument and the principal plus interest should be sufficient to meet the payment obligation in June.

In practice, merchant hedgers are well aware of basis risk. In the example, the merchant loses from a rise in the copper price, but he can reduce the exposure of his hedge strategy to basis risk by taking a small long position in copper. This idea is behind the recommendation of some brokers that the merchant hedger should buy, as in the above illustration, March copper and sell June copper to equal dollar amounts rather than for equal physical quantities.

The simultaneous trading of a dollar and British pound interest-rate futures contract in the London International Financial Futures Exchange (opened in October 1982) has opened up a new type of arbitrage opportunity.[8] Suppose we are in January, and a trader is studying quotations on the floor of LIFFE for the March delivery of the short-term pound and dollar interest-rate futures contracts, and for March/June spreads in the pound/dollar futures markets. He may notice that a bunching of buy orders has developed for pound interest-rate futures and that scalpers are offering to sell, but at a high price[9] – as they must be tempted by the prospect of significant profit when the bunching of buy orders subsides. At the price at which scalpers are selling pound interest-rate contracts, the trader may notice that there was a high probability of profit for himself by selling March pound interest-rate futures contracts (possibly undercutting slightly the scalper's price) and offsetting these almost immediately by buying March dollar interest-rate futures and spreading March into June pounds (i.e. selling March pounds and buying June pounds).[10] A bunching of sell orders in the pound interest-rate futures market would lead to an arbitrage opportunity in the opposite direction.

Triangular arbitrage opportunity of the type described is less likely to occur in the dollar interest rate than in the pound interest-rate futures market, given that the dollar is more liquid than the pound interest-rate futures market. Scalpers in the dollar interest-rate pit can hope to dispose of inventory at a faster rate than their counterparts in the pound interest-rate pit: the arbitrageur, who outdoes the scalper by being prepared to dispose of inventories in other markets, makes a less favourable comparison in the dollar interest-rate pit (where conditions are more liquid than in the pound interest-rate or pound/dollar futures market) than in the pound interest-rate pit. In general, triangular arbitrage opportunity between three futures markets that form a market triangle is most likely to appear at the least liquid corner of the triangle.[11]

HEDGING AND SPECULATION IN FINANCIAL FUTURES

In principle the investor, in appraising the risk of his portfolio, should consider the probability distributions from which its real value (including the reinvestment of earnings) is drawn at various dates in the future – for example, 3 months, 6 months, 12 months and annually thereafter up to 4 years. In practice, the investor is likely to be most concerned with the distribution at one of those various dates. For instance, an investor who plans to make large consumption expenditures two years from now would be most concerned with the probability distribution for two years from now. Some investors have no precise idea about when they will spend from their portfolio. They may focus on a date four years from now, if this date represents a 'certainty equivalent' of the possible dates in the future at which the portfolio could be spent. The date of the probability distribution, on which the investor concentrates, is called the 'horizon date' of his portfolio.

Consider an investor whose horizon is four years from the present, and who has a large proportion of his portfolio placed directly or indirectly in long-life assets.[12] Our investor may be an entrepreneur in the areas of real estate and oil exploration. The value of his portfolio at the horizon date would be likely to be diminished if *ex ante* real rates of interest (and expected real rates of return on market investments) were to rise in the period up to the horizon date; his long-life investments would have decreased in attractiveness relative to those that were now available in the market.[13] In principle, our investor should be a willing purchaser of hedges against an unanticipated rise in *ex ante* real rates of interest.

The investor with a four-year horizon who holds a well-diversified equity portfolio is less subject to interest-rate risk than the entrepreneurial investor considered above, for corporations in aggregate (whose equities our investor holds) have a well-balanced maturity spread of investments and investment projects. The entrepreneurial investor can choose between two principal methods of hedging – one using the conventional bond markets and one using the financial futures markets.[14] In the bond market, the entrepreneur (or the corporation in which he has a controlling interest) could issue a long-term fixed-rate instrument and invest the proceeds in short-term instruments. In the futures markets, he could take short position in the short-term interest-rate contract. Let us consider these two strategies in turn.

Suppose at the time of entering into the long-life investment, the entrepreneur issued a ten-year fixed-rate bond, using the proceeds to fund a monetary portfolio. The exposure of the value of the portfolio at the horizon date (four years from the present) to fluctuations in the *ex ante* real interest rate would have been thereby reduced, but the strategy has three disadvantages. First, the entrepreneur is assuming an inflation risk; for if inflation were to fall below expectations he would suffer loss, even though the *ex ante* real rate of interest may not have changed. Second, in taking on long-term debt he must pay a margin to the lender which covers the cost of administering the loan and monitoring that the conditions of the loan covenant are fulfilled. Third, lenders may overestimate the risk of lending to the entrepreneur, given their lack of special knowledge about the business or the entrepreneur's special abilities, and require an unacceptable risk premium to be built into the interest cost to insure against the possibility of default.

As an alternative strategy to issuing long-term fixed rate debt, the entrepreneur could take a short position in the interest-rate futures market. The level of *ex ante* real interest rates at the horizon date is not independent of the level of *ex ante* real returns in the preceding period, especially towards its latter end. Thus the entrepreneur can hedge, albeit to a very limited and uncertain extent, the value of his portfolio at the horizon date against the then *ex ante* real interest rate being greater than is now expected, by taking a short position in an interest rate futures contract. He will probably choose a near rather than a far delivery month, despite the closer dependence of the *ex ante* real interest rate at the horizon date on immediately preceding rather than on much earlier rates, because profit from far-distant contracts is subject to inflation risk that dwarfs probable variation in *ex ante* real interest rates. The correlation between profit on a short position in a near-term interest-rate contract and deviation of *ex ante* real interest rates in four years' time from their now expected level is likely to be small. In an inflationary environment, neither fixed-rate bond issues nor futures trading are of much help to the entrepreneur who seeks to reduce the effective maturity of his portfolio so as to bring it closer to his horizon date.[15]

Consider next the investor who holds a money and bond portfolio, and who again has a horizon date four years into the future. If there were zero risk of inflation, the individual described could reduce to near zero the variance of his portfolio's value at the horizon date by concentrating his investment in four-year fixed-rate bonds. Every six months he could roll over his bond portfolio (now reduced to having a maturity of only $3\frac{1}{2}$ years) into a new four-year bond portfolio.[16] But should there be a significant inflation risk, this matching of maturity of instruments with the horizon date would subject the investor to considerable risk. Instead his lowest risk portfolio is likely to be a combination of shorter term bonds and long positions in interest-rate futures. To demonstrate this, it is necessary first to recognise an equivalence between a bond and a position in futures.

A four-year fixed-rate bond, for example, is equivalent to a three-month bill (issued today), plus equal value long positions in three-month interest-rate futures contracts with delivery months at three-month intervals up to three months short of four years. The investor with a four-year time-horizon must decide under different inflationary conditions on the optimum distance into the future for which to buy contracts, and for what total value. Only under conditions of very low inflation risk would his minimum risk portfolio be composed of equal positions in all futures contracts up to four years ahead – the equivalent of an investment in four-year fixed-rate bonds.

The investor with the four-year horizon would be exposed to considerable risk if he simply bought three-month bills and took no position in futures contracts or longer term bills. For the *ex ante* real rate of interest can fluctuate considerably from one three-month period to the next, and the cumulated value of real income by the horizon date could lie within a wide range. In constructing his minimum risk portfolio, the investor would buy futures contracts for each delivery month into the future for which inflation risk (as seen from the present) is less than *ex ante* real interest-rate risk. As the investor looks into the future, inflation risk is likely to grow at a faster rate than *ex ante* real interest-rate risk; at some date, say for the delivery month one year from now, inflation risk may exceed *ex ante* real risk. The investor would not buy futures contracts for beyond that date. He may, however, buy futures contracts for a prior date to a greater value than that of his position in cash bills. This he would do if the *ex ante* real interest one year from now was very dependent on the level of the *ex ante* real rate in the earlier period, yet inflation risk (as seen from the present) could grow sharply between nine months and one year into the future. Then the investor's portfolio would be composed of say $1 million in one-year bills (equivalent to $1 million in three-month bills, plus long positions of $1 million in futures for delivery months 3, 6 and 9 months from now), plus an extra amount in futures for a delivery month six or nine months from now to hedge against a fall of the *ex ante* real rate in the period starting more than a year ahead.

As time progresses, the investor and his four-year ahead horizon move forward. After perhaps three months, he would roll over his bills and futures contracts, selling the bills which now had only nine-month lives and placing the proceeds into one-year bills; simultaneously he would liquidate his positions in interest-rate futures contracts now for a delivery month only six months ahead, and take out an equal long position in the delivery month nine months ahead. As a proxy to this type of roll-over strategy, many investors construct their money and bond portfolio by laddering maturities. For example, the investor may ladder his portfolio by dividing it equally between bills of maturities stretching with three-monthly gaps from three months ahead to two years. The composition of the portfolio is held constant. When after three months the present holding of three-month bills matures, the proceeds would be placed in a new two-year bill. The laddering technique, however, leaves the investor more exposed than does the earlier strategy to interest-rate risk; a significant portion of his portfolio would be invested in instruments of less than one year maturity, and so he would not be taking advantage of what hedging opportunities are available against *ex ante* real interest-rate fluctuation. Even so, where transaction costs are considerable, the laddering technique may be the most suitable.

The existence of financial futures markets allows the investor to gain protection against *ex ante* real interest-rate risk without assuming credit risks. Rather than the investor purchasing a one-year commercial bill (or placing funds in a one-year bank deposit) he could obtain the same degree of interest-rate protection by buying three-month CDs or commercial bills, and buying CD or T-bill futures for delivery 3, 6 and 9 months from the present. Yet the second strategy exposes him less to the credit risk of the commercial bill or CD issuer, for T-bills are of constant zero risk of default, whilst CD futures are of constant almost zero risk due to the monthly update of eligible names that can be delivered.

So far we have been considering the exposure of the investor to interest-rate risk which is attributable simply to the maturity of his portfolio being different from that of his horizon. But in addition the investor may be exposed because enterprises in which he has an equity interest are in interest-rate sensitive areas of the economy. For example, construction companies gain from a fall in real interest rates that is not expected to be reversed over the short or medium term. Cash inflows from property investment stretch typically much further into the future than for most other areas of investment, and as a lowering of interest rates raises the net present value of investments of long duration relative to those of short duration, a higher proportion of acceptable investment projects are found in the property sector when interest rates are low rather than when high. Construction activity and the profitability of construction companies should be boosted by a lowering of real interest rates. An entrepreneur who had a large proportion of his portfolio in the construction industry – or an allied industry such as brickmaking – could reduce the risk of his wealth-holding by hedging against a rise in real interest rates. As already discussed, financial futures markets offer scope – albeit very limited under inflationary conditions – for the hedging of real interest-rate risk.

An analogy can be found for the above type of economic exposure to interest-rate risks (in contrast to exposure that is due to a mismatching of maturities of instruments and the investor's time horizon) in the literature about hedging foreign exchange risk. The most usual type of exposure described is accounting; the accounting measure of exposure is the total mismatch between currency denomination of identifiable liabilities and assets.[17] In contrast, economic exposure to exchange risk refers to potential loss of net present value due to the adverse effect on long-run profitability of a change in exchange rates. For example, an oil company extracting and selling oil from the North Sea (in the British sector) would suffer a long-run diminution of profitability from a permanent real appreciation of the pound, given that its costs are largely UK-based, whilst its product is a dollar or SDR-commodity.

Banks have an economic exposure to interest rates, measured in nominal rather than in real terms. Where a bank has a sizeable amount of sight deposit business, and forces of competition are weak, profitability is likely to be positively correlated with the level of interest rates. The bank described can hedge its economic exposure to interest-rate risk by taking a long position in interest-rate futures, or by investing in a fixed-rate bond portfolio. It may be argued that a large bank whose equity is widely held could tolerate swings in profitability due to swings in interest rates. But a principal product which banks market is deposits, and these must be seen to be of extremely low risk, as they are bought by many small savers for whom they represent a large part of their portfolio. The risk of deposits can be reduced by smoothing out the rate of profitability over time by use of bond or of interest-rate futures markets.

Economic exposure to the movement of interest-rate differentials as well as to that of the absolute level of interest rates may be identified. For example, a bond-house specialising in selling bonds to retail investors may find that its turnover (and profitability) is depressed at times when the yield curve is downward sloping; the retail investor may show less interest in acquiring bonds when they yield less than short-term deposits. The bond-house could hedge its economic exposure by buying far-distant CD futures and taking a short position in near CD futures; this spread position would show a profit if the yield curve became less steep upwards than now forecast.

Economic exposure to fluctuation of the interest-rate differential between T-bills and CDs may be identified. For example, a widening of the differential (in favour of CDs) may be associated with heightened concern about potential bad debts in bank portfolios. Banks would find their profitability squeezed, as they could not pass their higher cost of funds (reflecting their deteriorated credit status) on to their top clients, who can raise finance directly from the market. A period of adjustment would follow during which banks would reduce their growth rates or contract, as they restored their ratio of capital to deposits to normal levels. A bank could hedge its profits against the emergence of a banking crisis by spreading CD futures against T-bill futures – taking a short position in CD and long position in T-bill futures for the same delivery month. The position would show a profit if the differential between CDs and T-bills widened. An alternative hedging strategy, which creates an identical position to that achieved by the futures trading, is to match longer term CD issues with the purchase of long-term T-bills.

Some firms have a straight accounting, in contrast to economic, exposure to the risk of fluctuations in the interest-rate differential between CDs and T-bills. For example, many firms in the USA that are active in commodity futures markets have large portfolios of T-bills, which they place, as an alternative to cash, as margin against their open positions.

They would prefer, if it were not for exchange rules stipulating that T-bills are the only alternative margin deposit to cash, to hold a smaller portfolio of T-bills and a larger portfolio of other securities, including CDs in particular. The excess amount of T-bills compared to CDs that they hold due to margin requirements may be termed their accounting exposure to the T-bill/CD interest-rate differential. By selling T-bill futures and buying CD futures they can hedge their portfolio against loss of income (relative to the level of income enjoyed if their portfolio had been free of margin constraints) due to a widening of the T-bill CD interest-rate differential.

We have taken as our principal example in this section an investor who has a portfolio composed of money, bonds and sometimes equity (and enterprise) investments. Many investors, including those in corporate form, however, are levered, with their debt outstanding exceeding their holding of money and bonds. Take for an example an entrepreneur, again with a four-year horizon, whose company has a large amount of floating rate debt outstanding where the interest rate is refixed at six-monthly intervals. Suppose that three-month *ex ante* real interest risk is greater than inflation risk (as seen from the present) up to a period starting nine months from now. Then the investor can reduce his portfolio's risk (measured with reference to the four-year horizon date) by dealing in the three-month interest-rate futures markets to cover nominal interest-rate exposure up to a three-month period starting nine months from now. Thus, just after the roll-over rate has been fixed, the entrepreneur sells three-month interest-rate futures for a delivery six months ahead; he may take a bigger position than in the underlying loan if indeed the futures contract can hedge *ex ante* real interest rate further into the future.[18] After three months have elapsed, the entrepreneur takes an additional short position in an interest-rate futures contract with delivery month nine months from now (and so he has a short position now in both six- and nine-month futures contracts). After six months, his loan rate is refixed, he takes out a new position in futures contracts nine months from now, whilst closing out all other positions.

Speculation in Interest-rate Futures

Interest-rate futures markets do provide increased flexibility for the speculator to back views about the level of interest rates in the future. Prior to the innovation of futures markets, the speculator on interest rates operated principally in the medium-term money and bond markets. The bill speculator who believed that interest rates would fall sharply could buy fixed-rate bonds or medium-term bills and fund his position by borrowing in the short-term money market. The bill speculator who believed that interest rates would rise sharply could issue fixed-rate bonds or borrow at a fixed rate from a bank and place the borrowed funds in short-term paper. These speculative procedures, particularly the second, were likely to be expensive both to arrange and to liquidate. The introduction of a financial futures market with its features of a central clearing house, standardisation and margin require-ments has allowed considerable cost savings to the outside speculator – the speculator who does not have great ma-noeuvrability due to existing commercial relations with banks and bond-houses.

Speculators in the interest-rate futures markets are likely to operate with a much shorter time horizon than those in the foreign exchange market (although not necessarily than those in the currency futures sector of the foreign exchange market). Most long-term speculation has as its basis a view about a real variable over the medium or long run: uncer-tainty about the rate of inflation and thus about nominal variables (for example, the nominal exchange rate or nominal interest rate) increases sharply as we look further into the future, whilst uncertainty about a real variable (for example, the real exchange rate or real interest rate) increases at a much slower rate as we look further into the future. Real exchange rates and real interest rates are tied to the anchors respectively, albeit loosely, of purchasing power parity and marginal efficiency of real capital investment. Inflation, by contrast, is tied to no anchor. It is possible in the currency markets to design a strategy for profiting on a view about the medium or long-term movement of the real exchange rate without usually assuming great inflation risk; it is not possible, in contrast, to design a similar strategy for real interest-rate speculation.

To demonstrate the above proposition, let us consider the case of currency speculation first. Suppose a speculator believes that over the next two years the mark will appreciate by around 10% in real terms against the US dollar; yet there is considerable uncertainty about the inflation differential between Germany and the USA the further the speculator looks into the future. Taking the estimate of the inflation differential, it could be calculated that the mark would be 7% higher in nominal terms than now is quoted for delivery in the two-year outright forward market. If the speculator simply sold dollars short for marks, in a two-year outright forward contract, the (subjective) probability distribution from which the profit would be drawn would have a substantial variance.

Closer examination of the nature of the two-year forward mark/dollar contract suggests an alternative speculative strategy, less subject to inflation risk. A purchase of marks under a two-year forward mark/dollar contract (entered into today) is equivalent to a purchase of marks under a three-month forward mark/dollar contract entered into today, plus the simultaneous entering into of three-month forward-forward contracts with delivery dates at three-monthly intervals up to 21 months hence; a three-month forward-forward contract with delivery month in June, for example, obliges the purchaser at maturity to enter into an outright three-month forward contract, with the forward premium on the mark set at the level specified in the original forward-forward contract. Forward-forward rates are closely related to the interest rate differential expected in the same three-month period, and this is highly subject to inflation risk, especially for far-off delivery periods. If the speculator eschewed the far-distant forward-forward contracts and simply rolled over six-month outright forward contracts he would reduce his exposure to inflation risk.[19] He would, however, become exposed to a new risk – that the forward premium on the mark would have increased above the implicit forward-forward rate, quoted at the start of the strategy, due to a widening of the real interest-rate differential between the USA and Germany. For example, after six months (from the date when the speculator initiated his roll-over strategy), most other speculators may have come to share the same view and the dollar would have come under downward pressure; but the Federal Reserve may have acted to slow the pace at which the dollar loses 10% of its real external value, by pushing up the real level of dollar interest rates. Such a response by the Federal Reserve would reduce the profit reaped from the current outright forward contract, shifting more of the potential profit from the original correct view about the long-run path of the real exchange rate on to those who had taken positions in forward-forward contracts. Nevertheless, for freely convertible currencies, the potential profit sacrifice through such shifts of profit from the holders of short-term outright forward contracts to the holders of forward-forward contracts should be small; forward-forward rates are less sensitive than the spot exchange rate to changing expectations about the long-run real exchange rate.

Next consider another speculator who believes that the level of short and medium-term real interest rates will fall by 6 percentage points over the next 18 months. Putting in a personal inflation expectation, the speculator can calculate the level of nominal interest rates 18 months from now. Suppose this nominal rate is 7 percentage points less than the rate quoted on interest-rate futures for the delivery month 18 months ahead. A large expected profit would then exist from taking a long position in that futures contract; but the profit would be highly sensitive to inflation risk. In contrast with the currency example, however, a position in short-term contracts, rolling over these on maturity, would not be a promising alternative strategy. A financial futures contract for delivery 18 months ahead is not equivalent to a position in a short-term futures contract plus other secondary contracts. If say, after six months, the market came to share our speculators' view about real interest rates in twelve months' time, the price of all futures contracts (for different delivery months) would rise, with the rise possibly being accentuated for the further distant dates. The speculator would capture only a small amount of the total potential profit from a simple position in a short-term contract.

It would be unusual for the interest-rate speculator to have a strong view about interest rates 18 months from now, and be aware of a large difference between the immediate view and the futures rate for 18 months hence, without there also being a large difference, albeit smaller, between one present view and the futures rate for 15 months and 21 months from now. If the subjective probability distributions from which profits for each of these contracts are drawn have significant variance, and if the profits from each contract are not perfectly correlated, then the speculator should hold a portfolio of different delivery months of interest-rate futures, weighted most heavily to that delivery period where his profit expectations are greatest.

Speculative strategies may be effected in spreads as well as in simple futures transaction. For instance, a speculator in April may believe that by September the yield curve will have become much less steep than is now discounted in the structure of futures prices; this view may be based on a narrowing of the risk premium implicit in futures prices as investors' nerves become calmed by a period of interest-rate stability following a prolonged period of volatility. The speculator would seek to profit from this view by selling June futures and taking a long position in September futures. The profit or loss would depend on a change in slope of the yield curve, rather than in the absolute level of interest rates. Very often, however, a view on the shape of the yield curve will be based on considerations – such as the state of the business cycle – that would have a more powerful influence on the level of interest rates than on the shape of the yield curve. A speculator with a strong view of how the business cycle is progressing would usually take a position in the simple interest-rate futures contract rather than in a spread. Only the very small speculator, who has very limited capacity to assume risk, may back his view about business cycle developments by dealing in the spread rather than in the straight futures market.

Speculation in the interest-rate futures market has a more remote influence on spot interest rates than it has in the currency futures market on spot exchange rates. For example, suppose we are in April, and sentiment in the interest-rate futures markets (with the most active contract being for June delivery) swings towards bearishness (i.e. a sharp increase in interest rates is expected). Using the T-bill futures contract as illustration, the fall in T-bill futures prices is likely to open up a profit opportunity whereby arbitrageurs sell five-month T-bills in the spot market, buy five-month T-bills spot and sell them two months forward in the sale-and-repurchase market, and buy June T-bills. On impact, the action of arbitrageurs would tend to raise the yield on bills (and deposits) with maturities of more than two months and to lower the two-month sale-and-repurchase rate. But in the equilibrium adjustment to the selling pressure in the futures market the two-month sale-and-repurchase rate (or other two-month money-market rates) plays no part: a fall in the two-month rate does not in itself induce speculators to buy longer term bills or T-bill futures.

Speculators, however, look at the futures rate (or the implicit two months forward three-month T-bill rate) and compare this with what they expect three-month interest rates to be in two months from now, not with the two-month rate today. The latter is determined by expectations concerning the path of the Federal Reserve's intervention rate in the overnight Federal funds market over the next two months, and if these expectations are not influenced by the bearishness in the T-bill futures market, the equilibrium two-months rate does not adjust. Day-to-day Federal funds rate is almost completely under the control of the Federal Reserve; it is the rate of interest at which the Federal Reserve provides or withdraws marginal funds to the market. The two transactions of the arbitrageur in the sale-and-repo and bill markets respectively do not influence supply or demand of bank reserves, and therefore do not change the overnight Federal funds rate. A fall in T-bill futures prices may influence, however, sentiment among participants in the two-month and shorter term money markets (for maturities of over one week), leading them to expect higher overnight rates within their short-term horizon. Then one-week to two-month interest rates would also tend to rise, with the overnight rate remaining unaffected.

As a second-order effect, the rise in longer term T-bill yields (and other longer term money-market rates) may encourage some investors to switch out of currency into long-term T-bills or long-term deposits, and may cause some marginal commercial investment projects to be rejected, so reducing commercial borrowing demand; both reactions would create excess supply in the bank reserve market, and downward pressure on interest rates in the overnight market would develop. Thus bear pressure in the futures market would cause some slight downward move of very short-term interest rates, whilst pushing rates for all other maturities upwards. It is the longer term rates to which many real investment decisions and exchange market decisions (how much of a portfolio with a medium-term horizon) are sensitive, and so speculation in the futures markets can have significant influence on the real economy.

NOTES

1. The settlement price for a CD under the futures contract, whatever the maturity of the CD, is calculated by using a constant interest rate, based on the closing price of the CD futures on the day before delivery day. CD futures prices are quoted as an index, in analogous fashion to the prices of T-bill futures.
2. Note that the names of CDs that are deliverable can change from one month to the next. What is being compared here is the index price of deliverable CDs, whatever they may be.
3. During the delivery period the clearing house pairs sellers' and buyers' delivery commitments by matching the oldest long positions with the sellers' delivery commitments as received.
4. E.g. a three-month forward three-month CD rate can be calculated for any particular name from knowledge of the three- and six-month CD rates.
5. Net running cost of hedges inventory is sometimes termed *convenience rent*, and is the excess of financing and storage

costs over the contango (the premium of the forward price over the spot price).

6. The financing and storage cost of copper as quoted for March to June less the premium of the June over the March price of copper, where all these magnitudes are measured as % p.a., equals what is termed the convenience rent. See for example, L. G. Telser, 'Futures Trading and the Storage of Cotton and Wheat', *Journal of Political Economy*, 66 (1958) 233–55.

7. Convenience rent is expressed as a proportion of unit value.

8. The short-term dollar and pound interest-rate futures contracts in London are designed in similar fashion to the euro-dollar contract on the IMM. Settlements of the contract are based on an independent interest-rate index with no physical delivery. Delivery months and dates are synchronised with those in Chicago's IMM.

9. The price of an interest-rate futures is quoted as an index, where 100 minus the index equals the relevant interest rate.

10. This currency spread transaction could be effected alternatively in the traditional swap market, swapping dollars into pounds for June delivery and simultaneously swapping pounds into dollars for March delivery.

11. This proposition about triangular arbitrage in futures markets is weaker than the parallel proposition for decentralised markets in which there is continuous market-making. For the latter, efficient arbitrage at the least liquid corner should preclude arbitrage opportunity from ever appearing at the other two corners. See B. D. Brown, 'Triangular Arbitrage' in *A Symposium on Futures Markets*, ed. M. E. Streit (Oxford: Blackwell, 1983).

12. A long-life asset is one for which a large proportion of its present value is attributable to returns expected far into the future.

13. In one special situation, a rise in *ex ante* real rates of interest (and other market rates of return) would not be associated with a capital loss on the long-life asset. That would be where the net revenue from the project rose simultaneously with the real rate of interest, as a joint response to a spontaneous increase in the productivity of capital, due to a technological advance. The situation considered implicitly in the text example is where the real rate of interest rises for reasons other than spontaneous

rise in the marginal efficiency of capital (e.g. tightening monetary, easing fiscal policy, or a changed rate of time preference)

14. For simplicity, we continue to consider an investor who at this point has no debt outstanding.

15. The most effective way of reducing effective maturity without assuming great inflation risk would probably be the issue of indexed bonds.

16. It is assumed that the investor's horizon is always four years from the present; thus it is continuously being rolled forward as the investor passes through time.

17. Analogously, accounting exposure to interest-rate risk would be calculated by assessing the mismatch between the average maturity (measured with respect to frequency of interest refixing) of the corporation's financial assets and liabilities.

18. The argument here is analogous to that used earlier for the depositor. If *ex ante* real interest rates are highly correlated through time, and inflation risk increases the further we look into the future, then an interest futures contract for June may be the best hedge against real interest rate risk in September.

19. In principle, because the investor's horizon moves forward with him in time, he should keep the maturity of the outright forward contract constant. Thus after one month he closes out the existing contract, now with only five months to mature, and replace it with a new six-months contract.

4 Long-term Interest-rate Futures

The American Treasury bond market is the largest single fixed income market in the world, followed closely by the United Kingdom gilt market. Both are also considered to be the most efficient fixed income capital markets as well. By efficient is meant the relative ease with which new issues may be brought to market, as well as the ability of the secondary market to facilitate large trades without serious price disruption. It is almost natural, therefore, that fixed income futures instruments would necessarily be based upon instruments from these markets.

The fact that highly efficient capital markets provide futures hedging instruments is not paradoxical however. Any financial futures instrument which hopes to survive in the market-place must itself be liquid and this liquidity is based in part upon the liquidity of its underlying instrument. This is not to imply that all futures based upon well-traded cash bonds or notes have been successful. But it does point out that when volatility cannot be reduced by trading, a need immediately arises for a suitable means of mitigating risk. Conversely, if there is not enough volatility in certain areas of the yield curve then speculators will not find it worth their while to provide funds. But in all cases, the structural nature of the future must be in keeping with the basic trading premises of the cash markets.

The dollar denominated financial futures market in the long-term fixed income instruments is currently represented by four instruments – the four- to six-year note future, the

ten-year note and long bond future, and Government
National Mortgage Association futures (represented by two
types of contract). Experience to date indicates that only two
of these have proven highly successful. At the time of writing,
the British gilt future trading on the LIFFE is still in its
infancy.

When viewed in an overall context, including the money
markets, it becomes apparent that the most popular futures
contracts are those on US T-bills and long-term bonds,
representing the opposite ends of the yield spectrum. At these
opposite poles is witnessed the greatest volatility on the yield
curve. Because of their short lives, Treasury bill yields can be
seriously affected by a small movement in price. For instance,
a three-month bill yielding 9% will have its yield change
0.25% for a $\frac{1}{4}$ point movement in price. While the price
movement may seem small, the nature of the money market
and its various instruments can mean that other opportunities
can quickly present themselves at better yield levels. So a
small movement can have some serious consequences for the
short-term investor.

At the longer end of the yield curve a different sort of
volatility is evident. If a 13% bond with 15 years to maturity
moves $\frac{1}{4}$ point, the yield change would be only 0.05%. This
price/yield movement is superficially less serious than the
move in bill yields but is nevertheless troublesome because
traditionally long bond volatility is caused by major interest
rate movements rather than by aberrational hiccups of a few
hours or days. When long bond yields begin to move
substantially, especially if they deteriorate, hedging becomes
an obvious possibility. The comparative volatility among
various maturity dates of constant coupon can be found in
Table 4.1.

Since not all futures contracts on longer dated instruments
have lived up to expectations, a somewhat closer examination
of the cash markets is necessary in order to provide both
background material and a better understanding of how
traders and investors react to new instruments which may be
structurally out of step with their own interests or experience.

TABLE 4.1 Effect of $\frac{1}{4}$ Point Price Change on Bonds of Varying Maturity with 10% Coupon*

Price	1 Year	3 Years	5 Years	7 Years	10 Years	15 Years	30 Years
100	10.00	10.00	10.00	10.00	10.00	10.00	10.00
99	11.11	10.40	10.27	10.21	10.16	10.13	10.11
98	12.24	10.82	10.53	10.42	10.33	10.27	10.22
97	13.40	11.23	10.81	10.63	10.50	10.40	10.33
96	14.58	11.66	11.08	10.84	10.67	10.54	10.44
95	15.79	12.08	11.37	11.06	10.84	10.68	10.55
94	17.02	12.52	11.65	11.29	11.01	10.82	10.67
93	18.28	12.96	11.94	11.51	11.19	10.96	10.79
92	19.57	13.41	12.23	11.74	11.38	11.10	10.91
91	20.88	13.87	12.53	11.97	11.56	11.25	11.04
90	22.22	14.33	12.83	12.21	11.75	11.40	11.18

*Coupon compounded annually

THE US TREASURY BOND MARKET

Excluding Treasury bills of one year or less the US Treasury note and bond market extends out along the maturity spectrum from one to thirty years. The total outstanding capitalisation, in nominal terms, of this marketable debt is an estimated $496 billion (first quarter 1982). If bills are added, the total amount is some $753 billion. The average length of US Treasury debt has fallen since the Second World War, when it was about nine to ten years, to about four years today. This is due to several complicated factors but primary among them is the ever-increasing cash appetite of the Treasury for short-term money. And in recent years interest-rate volatility has made many investors wary of buying long-dated debt, so the natural outcome has been an increase in the shorter variety. For example, the interest-rate spiral caused by the first OPEC price rise resulted in the average length of privately held Treasury bonds/notes falling to a post-war low of about $2\frac{1}{2}$ years in 1975.

Outstanding bonds are found in every maturity year along the curve although in standard practice new bonds are issued with maturities at 2, 3, 4, 5, 7, 10, 15, 20 and 30 years. Treasury yields are the lowest in the universe of dollar bonds because the government remains the most highly regarded credit risk. As a result, their yields represent basic fixed income market opportunity costs; the numeraire against which all other fixed income instruments must be measured. This single fact underlines the utility of Treasury yields as essential hedging benchmarks.

All direct obligations of the US Government are referred to as 'Treasuries'. Many government agencies are also guaranteed by the government but this category is reserved for those issues raised for Federal budgetary purposes. All Treasury obligations are brought to market at prevalent yield levels; that is, issues priced close to par with coupons reflecting the current secondary market yields on outstanding obligations. To date the Treasury has not indulged in issuing variable rate notes, low coupon discount bonds or zero coupon bonds, techniques used with success in the corporate and eurodollar bond sectors.[1]

For purposes of classification, two- to five-year Treasury instruments are referred to as notes while the longer maturities are referred to as bonds. Occasionally issues up to ten years are sometimes called notes as well. All instruments, other than T-bills, pay interest semi-annually and interest is calculated on a 360 over 360 day basis.[2] All American bonds trade with accrued interest attached until the actual coupon payment date when they trade free of accrued. Prices on the bonds are quoted in 32nds of 1 per cent (0.03125) and the normal trading spread on all but very inactively traded bonds is usually $^4/_{32}$, or $^1/_8$ of 1 per cent.

THE NEW ISSUE PROCESS

When the Treasury decides to issue a new bond or note, the issuing process is somewhat different from that found in the corporate bond sector where new issues are underwritten by a group of participating investment banks. Because of the government's large borrowing programme this process must be relatively fast so that little overhang occurs in order not to congest the path for further issues.

The speed with which a new Treasury may be brought to market can be assisted or deterred by the futures market, given the maturity length of the new bond. This will be seen more closely below. In the past, many variations of new issue techniques have been used but in this section we will confine ourselves to the most popular and current method, known as the auction. Because of recent large federal budget deficits the Treasury's appetite for new money has been quite voracious and this once obscure process now requires wide-spread attention at times as a harbinger of the condition of the credit markets overall.

Treasury borrowings for any particular period are usually known in advance by the investment community since they are announced in official estimates. The gross number is only an estimated number which may or may not be exceeded. And the gross number, in itself reflective of the ever-growing federal budget, must be netted out against the maturing debt it is intended to replace so that a 'new money' figure is also apparent. On the face of it, a new issue of $5 billion gross and net would have a significantly different impact upon the market than one of $5 billion gross, $2½ billion net.

The actual auction process itself contains several different stages. Basically, there are three stages involved: the announcement of a new issue; the competitive allocation process; and immediate after-market trading. The futures market keeps abreast of all three.

In the first stage, the new issue itself is announced. Assume that a 12% thirty-year bond has been scheduled, to be auctioned seven days hence. The initial reaction in the secondary market will be twofold. First, it will look to the existing yields on long bonds and examine the supply situation, and second, it will attempt to quantify crudely the impact of the net amount being raised upon yields for the foreseeable future.

Most recently, this twofold consideration has been extremely important because the new issue Treasury market has been trading on a when-issued basis. In anticipation of the new issue actually being auctioned, market-makers and traders may trade the issue as if it were already a security, thus giving it an anticipated yield level before it enters the competitive bidding stage. This yield level can be a harbinger (but only to an extent) of the auction outcome since it presages investor reaction.

This 'grey' market is in itself a type of short-term forward market in that investors and traders are taking positions in anticipation of a new yield level. As in any when-issued market, their positions are only valid if the issue actually materialises. Money only changes hands after the auction process is completed and payment date reached.

In the second stage, the actual yield and coupon level are established. At this time, the investing public is asked to submit bids for the new issue. This buying group is the institutions that will sell the issue to institutional and retail investors. The results of the auction are carefully analysed. Assume that the results of the 12% thirty-year auction are printed in short form as the following:

TABLE 4.2 $2 Billion 12% 30-Year Treasury Issue

high bid	100.05 (11.99%)*
low bid	99.00 (12.13%)
average bid	99.90 (12.01%)
non-competitive awarded	$600 million
cover	2.5/1.00
average yield level	12.01%

* Yield to maturity, semi-annual

In Wall Street patois, a 'tail' of 0.14% is said to be evident here; the difference in yield between the high and low bid. The size of this gap can give a good indication of the relative success or failure of an issue. The non-competitive bid level means those bids that were submitted simply to buy the new issue but not at a specific level. The cover means the ratio of total bids versus the issue size; in this case $5 billion.

During this stage, the yield levels of existing long bonds can be under pressure as attention is focused on the new issue. If it becomes apparent that this issue will yield more than existing issues, some swapping may occur from old to new bonds. But equally important for the futures market is the relative price of this issue to others in the market for if its coupon is high as well as its yield it may then become the benchmark for the futures market; that is, the 'cheapest' bond to deliver against a short (see section on futures pricing below).

The last stage in this process is in some instances hardly distinguishable from the second. The new bond will normally become the bell-wether instrument in its range only if it has the highest coupon of bonds currently existing. In this respect, yield and market price is ignored simply in favour of coupon. However, in times of falling yield levels and premiums on high coupon issues, it is debatable whether the erstwhile bell-wether can maintain its position as the most examined bond in the market.

This somewhat simplified process illustrates how a new issue comes to market and also provides the background for futures to be used professionally by those at the institutional or wholesale level who may be at risk during the various stages. A dealer (investment bank/broker) is at risk during the immediate selling period for the issue and may find a version of the short hedge advantageous if rates turn against him. This could be the elementary short hedge or a more complex version involving spreading at different contract months. As we shall see in a section below, the percentage difference in futures prices on bonds is in fact the bond dealer's view of short-term interest rates. He may utilise these spreads to offset any adverse rate movements against his cash position.

THE GOVERNMENT NATIONAL MORTGAGE ASSOCIATION

The second type of long-term fixed income future in the United States is The Government National Mortgage Association (GNMA or Ginnie Mae) future. This was in fact the first long-term future to be introduced into the Chicago markets in 1975. Since that time it has proved extremely popular although, because of its somewhat complicated structure, it does not trade in as heavy volume as the long bond contract.

The agency itself was established in 1968 in order to, *inter alia*, provide financing for the originating of (for the most part) single family dwelling mortgages. In order to do so, the agency developed the GNMA certificate, itself mortgage backed and guaranteed by the full faith and credit of the government in case of default.

The type of instruments used by the futures market are not the only ones issued by GNMA but shall be the sole focus of attention here. They are more properly called 'pass-through' certificates and are quite different from Treasury bonds. Each certificate ultimately represents a pro rata share of pooled mortgages which in turn provides their backing. A GNMA is created when a mortgage institution or bank assembles a pool of mortgages at roughly similar maturity and presents them to a custodian bank. The agency then issues certificates against these pools.

The flow of interest and principal payments from the mortgage holders provides the stream of payments received by the investor. However, this in itself would not satisfy investors who were credit conscious so the obligations obviously become those of the agency. This serves to shift the credit risk from individuals to an institution which is ultimately guaranteed by the federal government.

The obligations are called pass-through certificates because the payments made by mortgage holders are aggregated and passed directly along to the security holder. This means that GNMA holders receive interest payments, as well as part principal repayment, on a monthly basis rather than semi-annually as do bond holders. Again, if this flow is interrupted the agency will be able to rely upon the government to make up any shortfall, thereby modifying the original process. Hence the origin of the instrument's full name, the GNMA modified pass-through certificate.

These obligations have a distinct advantage over US Treasury bonds for yield-conscious investors because they pay interest monthly rather than semi-annually.[3] But because of their modified nature they trade at a yield premium to Treasuries. The reason for this is not so much a credit consideration as much as one of potential lost opportunity. If the agency should need to invoke the government guaranty, the time lapse involved (perhaps one or two months effectively) would mean yield loss and investors would therefore expect the market to compensate for this potential time lag.

GNMA obligations, totalling some $130 billion at mid 1982, are not issued in varying maturities but in constant thirty-year maturities with an implied shorter life of twelve years. This average life *per se* is not reached through sinking fund provisions, as are most corporate bonds, but through the assumption that most long-term mortgages will be prepaid in less time. Therefore, shorter date GNMAs are simply those whose time is running down, not the results of a different issuing policy. However, there is a full range of coupon levels available depending upon when the issue was released.

The method of issuance is also somewhat different from that of the auction. When the mortgage institution deposits the pooled mortgages it originated with a trustee institution and eventually has a security written against it, a new issue has been originated. Subsequently the agency releases that new issue to the dealer network for sale. And for accounting purposes, since they are first and foremost agency obligations, they are not balance sheet items in so far as the federal government is concerned.

These obligations are some of the most difficult in the US fixed income market because of their complex nature. Because of this difficult structure, their yield relationship with long Treasuries is not a simple matter (see Figure 4.1). Recent experience has shown that their once historic yield spread over Treasuries should not be necessarily taken for granted. Although GNMAs are ostensibly thirty-year instruments, their shorter (on average) lives make them more akin to ten- to twelve-year bonds. But their relationship cannot be taken for granted because the twelve-year assumption is only an average assumption; some GNMA holders could be totally repaid in seven years, others in fifteen or twenty. In this respect they are quite similar to longer-term corporate bonds possessing mandatory sinking funds. But unlike the corporate bond holder who may find part of his holdings called in for mandatory redemption, the GNMA

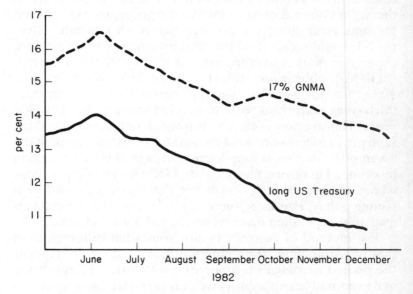

FIGURE 4.1 Long US Treasury Bond and GNMA Yields

holder will begin to receive a partial principal repayment in his monthly cheque along with interest payments. This occurs because it is highly improbable that all mortgage holders would decide to prepay their obligations at precisely the same time. However, the net effect for the GNMA holder and corporate bond holder is much the same; the bonds are susceptible to early repayment, and this only tends to confuse yield expectations.

Yields on GNMAs and Treasuries became seriously affected when interest rates began to fall precipitously in 1982 (see Figure 4.1). The spread between them widened as GNMAs failed to perform as well as Treasuries although a tandem price move ordinarily would have been expected. But the shorter-lived GNMA was struck by the same phenomenon that also affects many high coupon callable bonds when interest rates begin to drop. Investor preoccupation with the call price, especially if the bond is at a high premium, can cause it to trade at a yield premium to other issues with lower coupons either not possessing a call or having a call price which does not yet appear, in present terms, to deprive the bond holder of potential capital appreciation.

For most comparative purposes, GNMA pass-through obligations must therefore be considered comparable with long Treasury bonds for yield and hedging purposes. However, there are several instances in which their shorter lives could provide hedging opportunities with the sort of instruments mentioned above. This will be dealt with below.

TREASURY BOND FUTURES

The long-term Treasury bond future is based upon a notional 8% bond of twenty years maturity. When this contract was initiated, this was the general yield level for long bonds. Subsequently, although yields rose to a high of 14% the contract remained at the original coupon level although the price obviously dropped to a discount.

The contract has remained the most popular of the longer term futures although four- to six-year notes and a ten-year note contract were subsequently introduced. As its cash counterparts, it is traded on a ¹/₈ point spread on the exchange floor and its price is also quoted in 32nds of a point. Eventual delivery requires bonds not callable by the Treasury for at least fifteen years from the present so that the maturity date of the physicals has a minimum life-span.

Because the contract has been quoted at a discount for most of its trading life its basis with the cash market has been quite varied. In a more perfect world where futures and cash are quoted on essentially the same basis (suggesting similar coupons and maturities) the basis fluctuations are easier to gauge than when interest rates spiral, forcing older, lower coupons to a deep discount. Since bond yields rose dramatically since 1978, these new levels have meant that several adjustments have had to be made to both the mechanics of trading as well as the psychology of hedging.

On the mechanical side, discount futures prices plus the continuing supply of new long-term bonds have resulted in a great number of new issues being added to the deliverable list. In reality, very few older issues are still considered contract grade. But more importantly those familiar with the Treasury market will note that a twenty-year bond (regardless of coupon) is not the sort of maturity traditionally referred to as a 'long bond' in market patois. This is usually reserved for the thirty-year issues.

This discrepancy is adjusted in two ways. The contract calls for delivery of a bond with a fifteen-year 'requirement'; that is, a bond with at least fifteen years left to maturity. If, as said before, the bond is callable, its true life must be at least fifteen years.[4] Any issue under this period is excluded and any over it is included.

How then are adjustments made to the sundry long bonds to determine their suitability if, in the event, an actual delivery is necessary? Imagine that you have a short position and that you must deliver bonds to the long. Each individual eligible bond in the market will have a different price and you must deliver ten lots ($1 million nominal) to the clearing house. In order to determine how many bonds of any particular type must be delivered you must employ the adjustment factor.

This is a method whereby you can tell exactly how many

bonds to deliver as well as determine which issues in the market represent relative 'cheapness' for this purpose. The formula for the factor is:

$$\frac{\text{price of bond}}{100} = 8\%$$

regardless of the coupon level of the particular bond in question. The simple arithmetical calculation is thus carried forward into another, fuller calculation. But it becomes obvious here that the higher the price, and necessarily the coupon, the higher the factor will be.

Continuing the example, assume that you decide to examine the suitability of the highest coupon bond in the long maturities; now the 14% of November 2011. The reason for choosing to examine it is that, as the highest coupon, it also happens to be the highest yielding bond at the time. In order to determine the invoice amount of bonds you must deliver, the following calculation would then be used:

futures settlement price × nominal amount × conversion factor = principal   amount + accrued   interest = invoice amount

This calculation is valid for both types of bond future currently traded, the ten-year note and the long bond (as well as the presently defunct four- to six-year note). It also applies to the actively traded GNMA contract. A more practical example of how this calculation produces the cheapest bond to deliver will be outlined in the section on futures pricing later in this chapter.

Within the original calculation for the factor above, and therefore implied in all other formulae using it, is a very subtle yet significant distinction which differentiates bond futures trading on the CBT and IMM from other varieties, notably the GNMA CD future and the now defunct NYFE bond future. Since the factor here is derivation of the price of a bond yielding 8% to match the futures coupon, it is not the same as imputing a present value to a bond using the futures yield as a guideline. When the factor is multiplied by the product of the

contract nominal amount and futures settlement price the
result is the amount of principal of the particular bonds under
scrutiny which must be delivered. Thus, futures which use
such a method are known as *principal maintenance* contracts;
they use a factor based upon the price of any particular bond
to determine the amount of bonds deliverable against a
contract. Yield to maturity never directly enters the calculation.

TABLE 4.3 Adjustment Factor to Yield 8%, US Treasury Bond
Futures

term in years	coupon rate			
	12³/₄	13	13³/₄	14
30	1.5373	1.5656	1.6504	1.6787
27	1.4399	1.5498	1.6323	1.6598
25	1.4296	1.5371	1.6176	1.6445
23	1.4177	1.5221	1.6004	1.6265
21	1.4037	1.5046	1.5803	1.6056

The other method of determining the invoice amount of
bonds to deliver is illustrated by the *yield maintenance*
contract. This calculation approaches the problem somewhat
differently. The arithmetic is approached in two steps, as
follows:

1. Calculate the yield on the futures contract, using notional
   coupon level as real level and notional number of years to
   maturity as maturity end date. Use the futures closing
   price as bond price.
2. Take the yield level given as answer and use it to imply a
   present value to the particular bond in question.

Whereas the principal maintenance contract ignores yield to
maturity, this method incorporates it into both stages. The
results can be very different if one were to calculate both
methods for a single bond. But since both recent contracts
using yield maintenance are presently defunct the differences
are somewhat academic at this point. However, we shall

return to the matter of yield alone as a determinant of cheapness in another section below.

The six-year Treasury note future also uses the now standard principal maintenance method but cannot be considered a valid contract. It has been ignored by both traders and investors alike because it represents a point in the maturity spectrum not volatile, as are the short and long ends. This is in antithesis to what otherwise may appear as the basis for a flourishing business; in mid-1982 there were some $57 billion outstanding of notes in the four- to six-year range as stipulated in contract delivery terms. This represented about $14\frac{1}{2}$% of all notes due between 1982 and 1992. This figure was actually higher than the long-term Treasury notes whose contract calls for delivery of a $6\frac{1}{2}$-year bond at the first day of delivery month. The figure for such notes was an estimated $38 billion. Long-term Treasury bonds themselves, of deliverable quality against the bond contract, had only $55 billion outstanding.

Why then the failure of the four- to six-year note, the moderate success of the ten-year bond or note, and the continued strong success of the long bond contract when outstanding nominal amounts seem to suggest a different picture? For the most part, the answer has to do with volatility and medium-term instruments are not worth hedging because of their less volatile nature. But more importantly is the highly speculative nature of the floor market where phlegmatic instruments stand little chance of success.

GNMA FUTURES

Ginnie Mae contracts are not quite as straightforward as Treasury bond contracts because of the somewhat complex nature of the underlying cash instruments. Two types of contract exist for GNMAs although at present only one has proved successful over time. Perhaps more than Treasury bonds, GNMAs illustrate the vast problem that volatile interest rates can cause.

A GNMA contract is based upon a pool of mortgages

presumed to yield 8% for a life of thirty years. As already mentioned, an assumption is made that these thirty-year securities will be, on average, prepaid in twelve years; an assumption that causes some serious distortions in trading price and yield relationships with other markets.

The two types of contract have similar and quite confusing names – the collateralised depository receipt (CDR) and the certificate delivery (CD, not to be confused with the money-market instrument). It is the CDR which has proved the viable contract although the nature of the CD points to some frailties of GNMAs in general.

The name CDR implies that it is not GNMAs themselves which are deliverable against the contract, but a certificate witnessing GNMAs deposited with a bank and that the receipt itself is substituted for physical security delivery. This avoids the physical problems of transfer and avoids several problems encountered by the CD.

Both contracts call for the same notional security to be delivered and both also make another implicit assumption, that an 8% security yields 7.96% rather than its face value at par. This is based upon the fact that GNMAs pay their first monthly interest forty-five days after the security is first issued and then monthly thereafter. This initial period is carried forward and there is then an interest free delay of fifteen days.

The principal maintenance concept is used for GNMA CDRs but not for the CD, which instead is based upon a yield maintenance calculation. This contract calls for actual securities to be delivered to a specific depository. But the cumbersome problem for this contract was the yield main-tenance which has a 'par cap' stipulation. This means that securities priced above par cannot be delivered against the contract. Only the most current securities being issued are exempt from this. In effect, it prohibits all secondary market issues priced above par (those with high coupons) from being delivered. In periods of high interest rates this can seriously affect the number of deliverable bonds available in the market-place.

One of the thornier questions raised by GNMA cash securities is the shorter than thirty-year life-span. This is especially difficult for the deliverer of bonds against a short because the pools of mortgages are changing all the time and this can materially affect the principal amount that has to be delivered. The solution to this problem has been the introduction of a ban, or tolerance limit, on the CDR contract of ± 2.49 per cent. The seller may deliver ± 2.49 per cent of the principal amount for delivery, in a uniform balance.

This is one technique for adjusting for the pay-downs which inevitably occur after these securities come into existence. But a broader problem still remains concerning cash pricing and yields.While this does not particularly affect traders or participants strictly within the GNMA market it does affect those who may use the futures to hedge in another market. If one were cross-hedging, what assumptions can one make about GNMA yields? Are they thirty-year or twelve-year yields?

Although it is tempting to think of them as twelve-year bonds, their price/yield relationship is still most closely akin to, and mainly monitored with, the long Treasury bond. However, their traditional yield spread at 100–150 basis points above long Treasuries can make them similar in a yield sense to some intermediate term corporate or eurobonds. But the interest-rate peregrinations of 1978–82 have thrown many historic yield relationships between different issues awry, especially as interest rates finally begin to plummet. This can be seen in Figure 4.1. As rates began to fall, GNMA cash yields did not follow suit. The major reason was that the combination of high coupon yields plus prepayment options made investors shy away from these issues, assuming that their high yielding investment would shortly begin to dwindle as principal repayments flowed through along with their monthly interest payment. In this respect, GNMAs were treated in much the same way as a callable bond, when the market price is above the call price. Certain investors then disassociate themselves from such issues, even on a total return basis. In the case of GNMA, this problem can become even more acute since investors do not have a specific call price or date they can refer to, only a vague twelve-year option. Thus, yields can languish at times when other yields behave more predictably. Ironically, the phenomenon originally hurting the viability of the CD contract later made itself felt in GNMA cash market yields.

THE UK GILT MARKET

The British gilt market is the second largest bond market in the world. It is also one of the oldest; as early as the seventeenth century various governments were selling debt issues to finance wars against the French. Over the years it has taken on its own distinct characteristics. Many gilt market terms are more familiar to stockbrokers than other bond people because the London Stock Exchange has been the traditional home of the gilt market.

The term 'gilt' is a nickname for British government stock. For those not familiar with British terminology this means a bond, not a share. Gilts are so referred because they represent the highest rated credit risk in the country. Unlike their American counterparts, gilts do have a central trading location and this, plus other structural peculiarities, helps make the market arguably one of the two most efficient capital markets in the world.

The closest link that gilts have with the stock exchange is the government broker; the individual responsible for overseeing new issues to market. This person is himself a member of the broking community and his own personal functions are akin to those of other stockbrokers. Additionally, another even closer functional link can be found through the jobbing system, which acts for gilts as well as ordinary shares. Between these two functions we shall see how a new issue comes to market and is sold.

Gilts, like American government bonds, extend from one year to thirty-odd years to maturity. The distribution of maturities along the yield curve is broken down into fairly traditional terminology, with shorts (3 months–5 years), intermediates (5–15 years) and longs (15–30 years). Shorts especially have an added significance in the market because of the nature of British T-bills. No bill is issued for more than ninety days, so a large vacuum is left between three months and one year which is filled by existing issues running down to maturity. This is not to imply that there is a dearth of suitable instruments in the money market, since there is usually an adequate supply of one-year local authority (yearling) bonds and discounted trade bills, but the absence of long T-bills is conspicuous. Generally, shorts and intermediates account for two-thirds of all outstanding gilts.

In addition to the usual redeemable sort of bond, there is a small category of non-redeemables in existence in the market. These are bonds with low coupons that trade at a deep discount from par value. Sometimes the term perpetual is used to describe them since they have no ostensible maturity date. What this actually means is that they are redeemable, but only at government option. The option would not appear likely in most circumstances. The most popular of them, the War Loan is paid interest free of tax. All other gilts pay interest semi-annually (360/360 basis) net of the basic rate of withholding tax, except in a limited number of cases where overseas investors receive the full coupon.

The most important differences between the gilt market and the American government market is found in the method of issuing and secondary market trading. Central to this difference is the role of the jobbers in trading; those persons who maintain a market in the numerous issues traded. Jobbers, whether they trade shares or gilts, maintain the two-way price system of bid-ask quotations on the Stock Exchange floor. But in keeping with what is known as the single capacity system they do not deal with the public; this role is reserved for brokers. Neither do brokers make markets under this system; they only deal for their clients. The separate functions help to ensure that one person does not make a market and act as broker in the same issue.

All gilt trading is directed to the floor of the London exchange where it is executed by jobbers for brokers. Spreads involved are normally narrow and are in line with those made in the US Treasury market ($^1/_8$ point). London's reputation as an efficient capital market derives, as does the American reputation, from the fact that relatively large orders can be executed without materially affecting the price of the stock involved. While this does not necessarily satisfy what is known as the theory of capital market efficiency, it does nevertheless embody its spirit by at least confirming that profit is not possible by manipulation, since the various functions of the market are too well organised and controlled for such things to occur ordinarily.

METHODS OF NEW ISSUES

Announcements of a new issue are normally made on Friday afternoons. The terms of the new stock are given and the issue enters a tender period. The tender method is quite similar to the auction process used in the US government market. Prospective buyers submit a bid at which they wish to purchase the stock, subject to a minimum price. Preference will thus be given to the highest bids, normally allocated in full provided they are above the minimum accepted price.

As in any bond market, new issues are priced according to yields in comparable outstanding secondary paper in the market. However, as we have already seen in outline in the case of the Treasury auction, there is no guarantee against a 'tail' developing during the tender process. Although this situation cannot be prevented, one variation of the tender does exist which can help a new issue along, especially when demand is low in times of economic uncertainty.

Traditionally, fixed income investments provide the investor with little speculative appeal because of an absence of a gearing or leverage factor. However, the gilt market has successfully used a *partly paid* method of issuance which has some speculative appeal and has undoubtedly attracted investors to tender as a result.

Under this system a new stock is announced, as above, with one further nuance; it is only partially payable upon subscription. For example, 25% of the nominal value of the stock (£100 in the standard case of gilts) is due in three weeks with the balance not due for six months. However, as beneficial owner of the stock, the investor has full benefit of any capital gain that may ensue due to favourable interest-rate movements. Any rate improvement can thus be capitalised upon for a fraction of the nominal price. Since no margin accounts exist in Britain this method has proved something of a short-term substitute. In the same vein interest is paid on the partly-paid amount, on a proportional basis.

Whether or not this gearing ability will detract from the gilt futures contract remains to be seen. In theory it should not because futures contracts provide the ultimate leverage for investors. Unfortunately, there is no American precedent here for partly-paid stocks do not exist in the Treasury market.

The partly-paid stock period thus resembles an elongated type of account trading as used in the stock market. It has also been successfully borrowed by the eurodollar and euroster-ling bond markets. This is also true of another technique used in the gilt market; that of the tap stock.

In the event investors do not fully take up a new tender, the residue is booked by the government and re-offered for sale at a better price in the future. This then becomes the 'tap' nature of the stock. Its *raison d'être* is to help ensure that the balance of the new issue is not inauspiciously dumped in the market, thereby having a negative effect on secondary yields. However, a tap is not an afterthought following a poorly received issue; it is announced as such beforehand. If subscribers tender for the entire issue successfully then the tap may be fully exhausted. If not, it is held in government coffers for a better day.

The gilt market also possesses several types of instrument in addition to the traditional straight bond. A variable rate stock is similar to a floating rate note in that its semi-annual payments are linked to an indicator rate plus a fixed margin over it. Normally, the indicator is the T-bill rate and the margin $\frac{1}{2}$%. This is designed for investors who like to keep abreast of inflation by pegging themselves to volatile short-term rates. Most recently a new gilt was introduced which pegs itself at 2–2$\frac{1}{2}$% above the retail price index and is known as the index-linked issue.

Another innovative type of gilt is the convertible issue. This is a short or medium-termed issue giving the investor the right to extend his maturity into the longer term on predetermined terms, thereby playing the yield curve if interest rates should begin to fall. It should be noted that only straight gilt issues are deliverable against the gilt long-term futures contract; the hybrid issues do not qualify as deliverable securities.

THE LIFFE GILT CONTRACT

Trading in gilt futures began on the London International Financial Futures Exchange in November 1982. Because of the structure of the gilt cash market, the new future gave many market participants an ability they had not previously possessed; they could now sell a gilt short. The original membership of the Exchange reflected this. Most of the seat-holders were financial institutions while the individual speculator or scalper was not as prominent as he was on the floor of the Chicago exchanges.

The gilt contract is similar to the long Treasury bond contract with only one or two minor wrinkles differentiating them. The gilt future represents a 12% British government stock of twenty years to maturity. Its trading lot is similar to those of most US bond contracts – £50,000 per contract. It is also quoted in 32nds of a point. The twenty-year (average) maturity actually represents bonds with maturities of not less than fifteen years and not more than twenty-five years so it excludes the very long maturity dates. On this basis it represents that part of the yield spectrum where an approximate 25% of outstanding gilts lie.

In delivery terms, the gilt contract is more properly a principal maintenance contract, using the factor adjustment method. The factor itself is arrived at in the same manner as the US Treasury bond. In this case, it is as follows:

$$\frac{P(12)}{100}$$

where $P(12)$ equals the price per nominal value of the deliverable stock so that it has a yield to maturity (or gross redemption yield) of 12%. Once the factor is determined, the method of calculating principal amount due on any particular stock is the same as for the Treasury and the GNMA CDR.

When the gilt future began trading, it caused a phenomenon rarely seen before in financial futures markets – a contract actually trading at a premium. The relatively high benchmark yield of 12% was somewhat higher than prevalent yields at the time and the new contract opened at a premium. It was fortunate that the new contract was not a yield maintenance contract, for any sort of initial par cap or yield to call restriction could have seriously hampered its success even before it started trading.

The gilt contract is still in its infancy at the time of writing so it is difficult to speak of its future with any convincing certainty. Structurally, it has few apparent weaknesses in that it has been based upon the more successful type of American contract. But whether it will be able to win favour with both speculators and investors is another matter. Investors in Britain, regardless of their ultimate size, have been accustomed to a market where speculative investing is muted, normally manifesting itself in the stagging (short-term buying and selling) of new issues. And whether or not investor interest is complemented by speculative activity on the LIFFE floor will probably spell the eventual success or failure not only of this contract but of the exchange itself. Without the strong 'local' element on the exchange floor, liquidity will eventually disappear if the only desire of the institutional floor trader is to hedge his cash position and sell contracts short.

THE YIELD CURVE

On many occasions the most essential underlying factor providing the basic pricing model is often overlooked in futures markets, as trading techniques and mechanics often take precedence in both traders' and commentators' minds. While this is understandable given the complexity of futures markets it is not a valid reason for relegating the cash markets to a secondary position. This is perhaps no better illustrated than in yield curve considerations in the financial futures markets.

Not all futures pricing and trading are based upon yield curve considerations: often spreading strategies and arbitrage concentrate only on momentary anomalies in the market, regardless of the overall contour of the yield curve and expectations surrounding it. But no discussion of futures is complete, or even valid, without incorporating the yield curve because it is ultimately the volatility of the term structure of interest rates which provides hedging and speculative opportunities.

The yield curve is simply defined but has numerous permutations and subtleties surrounding it. Most simply it is the shape or contour of the line that graphically connects short-term to medium and long-term interest rates. As already mentioned, the US Treasury and UK gilt curves are the norms against which all other dollar and sterling yields must be measured; whether they be corporate, municipal or eurobond instruments.

The shape of the curve is perhaps the greatest preoccupation of financial institutions for it affects the continuing costs, and eventual success or failure of most financial activities. While there is ultimately no ideally shaped yield curve, from either a theoretical or historical perspective, there is nevertheless one from a practice perspective which is sometimes historically supported and which shall receive attention here.

Regardless of country or banking system one basic maxim holds true for any financial institution: in order to make a profit it must be able to fund its lending at a positive rate. In most cases, this means borrowing for shorter periods than one lends. This statement assumes that the slope of the yield curve is positive; that is, the rate at which one borrows will be lower than that at which one lends.

Under such conditions, a bank or other financial institution can borrow funds at six-month rates and lend for perhaps five years. The margin of profit would be the difference in nominal interest rates plus fees. With a positively sloped yield curve, a profit should ensue. What the bank is actually doing here is arbitraging the yield curve between two points. The problem is that this activity is not riskless in that it will have to borrow again in six months time in order to match its liabilities (borrowings) with its assets (loans).

The strategy only remains successful if short-term rates

remain lower than the longer term. If the yield curve should invert itself, turning to a negative slope, the profit margin is eradicated. Until the advent of financial futures, short-term rates quoted were obviously cash rates and little could be done to lock in present rates in the near future. But as the previous chapter has shown, it is now possible to use a variety of instruments to lock in present rates and, to an extent, protect oneself from short-term rate volatility.

What creates a positively sloped yield curve *vis-à-vis* a flat or negatively sloped one? Normally, this is answered in simple terms by invoking the all-mystical term 'investor expectations'. More specifically, a yield curve turns negative in periods when investors are unwilling to commit money to a long holding investment period when they can receive a better annual rate in the short term. Therefore, the combination of their activities plus the forces which clouded their expectations in the first place (usually price or money inflation) serve to push short rates higher than the others on the maturity spectrum by a type of demand-pull inflation of its own. In many instances, long-term rates become notional since a flight to the shorter yields leaves them in a general state of market illiquidity. They themselves can become extremely volatile because even a small amount of investor interest on a long bond can create a disproportionate swing in price/yield relationships.

Expectations must nevertheless be understood in an institutional context to appreciate the full effects of a negative yield curve. Two recent experiences in both the American and British cases will illustrate.

In the American example, short-term interest rates began to rise in 1978 and continued to new highs in 1981. While long-term rates rose concurrently, short-term rates were still higher in both absolute and real terms. Inflationary pressures and expectations were responsible but simultaneous changes in banking regulations also caused a shift in the savings behaviour of investors.

Traditionally, most savers channel their savings through accounts in banks or savings and loan associations. Under American banking law, simple savings accounts had an interest-rate ceiling placed upon the amount paid out. As short-term interest rates began their initial rise, due primarily to the impact of the second OPEC oil price rise, funds normally destined for these accounts began to be diverted into other vehicles, such as the newly created money-market funds, in search of higher yield. These new yields sometimes doubled or even trebled the return available on bank savings accounts. This flight for higher yield had the net effect of reducing some smaller banks deposit bases and whittling down the margin of profit many banks were enjoying on longer term loans.

This process is called 'disintermediation' and it has had a profound impact upon traditional banking structures and behaviour. It has proved conclusively that investors, and even those once thought to be passive, do seek high yield based upon their own expectations. But perhaps more importantly it signals an end to a banking practice which assumed for many years that its low interest, deposit paying base was secure.

The British example during roughly the same period was more subdued because banking practice was less restrictive and less disintermediation occurred. Deposit accounts in UK banks were not subject to the same restrictions as their American counterparts and their interest rates are instead tied to the banks' own base rate, itself a close parallel of the minimum lending rate.

These deposits found a willing home when lent out as short-term loans to a large cross-section of British industry. For a twelve-year period, between approximately 1970 and 1982, the British corporate bond market was to all intents and purposes defunct due to high long-term interest rates and a substantial amount of crowding out by the gilt market. Industry's immediate response was to borrow short on an almost continual roll-over basis. This served to put pressure on short rates, leaving the medium and long sectors of the yield curve to the government. This latter phenomenon also hit the US corporate market between 1979 and 1982 as high cost of medium and long borrowing forced many companies to borrow short, further skewing the yield curve as well as their own balance sheets.

As long as such structural abnormalities exist within the

banking system the yield curve will certainly come under pressure. If nothing else, these sort of phenomena serve to illustrate that yield curve changes are more than simply a matter of supply and demand without further qualification.

Earlier, interest-rate volatility among short and long dated maturities was mentioned. Table 4.1 illustrates that the long-dated bonds have a less significant yield change for $\frac{1}{4}$ point variations than do short or medium-term instruments due to the effects of these long lives upon the yield to maturity calculation. If a long bond and a medium bond were to yield Y_2 and Y_1 respectively on day one, the long bond would suffer a greater gross capital loss at the new level of Y_2 than would Y_1 at its new lower level. Put differently, the investor in the long-dated bond will have to wait for a significant readjustment in bond prices before his bond returns to the original price yielding Y_2. In either case the type of interest-rate movement necessary to create such a move will be more than a technical hiccup in rates. More likely, it would signify a distinct price adjustment caused by a cyclical shift in the trend prevailing originally.

Therefore, hedging long-term interest rates can be of significant importance even though the point for point volatility is less than that on shorts. While most discussions of rates tend to centre upon short rates and all the attendant industrial and social problems high rates can cause over time, long rates have their own special virtues which will be emphasised below.

THE REAL RATE OF RETURN

Assessing the value of a bond future *vis-à-vis* its underlying cash-deliverable instruments involves a host of mechanical considerations. But even before that can be adequately done one must have some measure of value for the cash instruments. How does one determine whether the yield on government bonds is adequate compensation for the time risk incurred? On another level, how does one cross the threshold between government and higher yielding corporate bonds on yield terms alone, and again by what criteria?.

There are many models existing which claim to measure the intrinsic value of bonds. Here we are only concerned with a concept which normally only raises its head in times of high inflation, when very natural questions begin to be asked about the yields on fixed income instruments. Do they provide an adequate return over the inflation rate? One answer lies in the real rate of return.

Different types of investors have various indifference levels concerning fixed income instruments. Many institutions managing fiduciary money must, for reasons of prudence, invest in government securities. Their assessment of return and risk thus appears to be based upon necessity rather than choice. But even within such a constricting framework, investors are still able to pick and choose among the various levels of yield available to them by actively managing their portfolios; that is by swapping or switching among similar issues by spotting anomalies, thereby enhancing cash flows and yields. This sort of process implies an underlying assumption about the relative value of the yields in question. This is not necessarily motivated by, but nevertheless involves, the real rate of return, or real (versus absolute) rate of interest.

The real rate is simply the yield of the instrument in question minus the inflation rate. Put another way, it is the income flow minus the expense of inflation. The net figure is the real amount of growth the investment provides. While the concept is simple enough, the various ways in which it can be measured are more complex and can significantly affect the final results.

On non-callable bonds two measures of yield are usually used – current (or running) yield and yield to maturity. The former is usually used as a precise indicator of cash flow but does not give a longitudinal value of a bond, factoring in discount or premium prices, as does yield to maturity. Now the return here is usually measured by using yield to maturity and it may be stated on an historical basis. But such assumptions about historical behaviour must also constantly use a standard measure of inflation. In the USA two are commonly employed, the GNP deflator and the consumer price index (CPI). The latter is the more popular because it is more easily understood than the deflator, which is the multi-variate basket used to net out the GNP figures announced quarterly. Due to the fact that CPI is announced monthly and is based upon a basket of goods more easily recognisable, it has gained more popularity. In many cases, it is also somewhat higher than the deflator, which in turn tends to monitor wholesale or producer prices.

In Britain, inflation is generally measured by the retail price index and an acceptable real rate has actually been designated by the introduction of the 2% index-linked gilt. When this particular issue was priced, that was the acceptable spread at the time and it was built into the new index-linked formula. In the USA, on the other hand, real rates touched a modern record high of almost 6% in 1981–2 before falling to a narrower margin. The large historic gap between bond yields and the CPI still did not draw investors into the bond market until it became apparent that inflation in fact had begun to fall.

Regardless of the measure chosen, the major problem with assessing the real rate is one of horizon. Price indices reflect the past trend while bond yields, on whatever basis, reflect the present return available. If an investor purchases a bond with six months to run until its next coupon then that present yield is also his future yield as well, at least for that period. More importantly, this illustrates that given the limitations of statistics and yields, investors are still left to their own devices to determine where interest rates and inflation proceed to next. In this respect, futures pricing can be an invaluable aid in such a market environment which necessarily tends to be one-dimensional. However, as we shall see, it is certainly not a panacea for the problem but rather only a looking glass.

Real rates of return are not as important as market expectations in assessing the suitability of fixed income investment. During the period following the Second World War until the late 1970s the American real rate (on long bonds) was negligible; sometimes not exceeding 1% and sometimes even negative. This long period stands in stark distinction to the rate realised in 1981–2 which ultimately fell but the rise in bond prices could not be attributed to the real rate alone.

YIELD SPREADS

In assessing the contour of the yield curve several practical considerations must be taken into account, both for the validity of theoretical conclusions as well as for the potential of cross-hedging; using futures to hedge non-Treasury or non-gilt positions. These centre around the types of bonds one compares to the curve or, put differently, the suitability of the government curve and futures in hedging different bonds. Essentially this boils down to investor indifference levels and how they reflect into market behaviour and procedures.

A basic underlying maxim of fixed income investor behaviour is often lost in the maze of arguments extolling the virtues of the futures markets; namely that even short hedging will not help increase an investor's threshold to risk. As an example, consider an investor who is bound to invest in the highest quality bonds. Superficially it would appear that futures may enable him to take on bonds of lesser quality and higher yield by protecting him against adverse rate movements.

The fundamental problem faced here would be the matter of basis (yield) risk; again, the amount of yield differential between the future (and its cash equivalent) and the lower quality bond. It is as important to note that this is not a static spread and is subject to change. In most cases, adverse interest-rate movements will do more harm to the lesser quality bond than to the benchmark.

For instance, the quality yield gap between the various gradations of credit risks can be charted historically in order to give an average spread between say AAA and A bond yields. Assume for a moment that this spread was, on average, 75 basis points over a previous five-year period. Is it possible for an investor to short hedge an A bond with as much as 100 basis points differential to lose on his position?

Generalisations about yield curve movements in the benchmark bonds should not necessarily be extended into all other bond sectors willy nilly. This is currently true more of the American rather than the British market because of the plethora of existing bonds. The reason that tandem moves should not be automatically anticipated is that, in times of economic uncertainty, credit concerns become paramount and will skew traditional yield levels from historical spreads.

If this traditional spread was established during a period not affected by recession, it would not be expected to remain in its old range once an economic downturn set in. In this situation, only the benchmark bonds would be expected to perform moderately well since their prices will be supported to an extent by a 'flight to quality'. An A issue would be under greater pressure in bad times as its profit margins or balance sheet come under the influence of a slowdown. Therefore, even if yields were to decline generally it should not be assumed that the A issue will immediately follow. It would be eminently possible to lose money at various stages of a short hedge here.

A host of other technical considerations can also come into play under such circumstances. Two of the most important to recognise for cross-hedging purposes are the effects of early call provisions and/or purchase/sinking fund provisions, both of which can affect the secondary market performance of their bonds.

Call provisions shorten the stated life should interest rates move in the borrower's favour. If the optional redemption is exercised by the borrower, the entire issue can be retired. However, if the bonds trade at a price premium to the call price, then investors will begin to calculate new yields, not reflecting current or redemption yield but yield to call. At a premium to call price, this yield is lower than yield to maturity. Thus, this sort of bond can be expected to under perform issues with no calls, especially in strong market environments. Hedging an issue of this nature can prove difficult, even if it is of the highest credit risk.

Purchase and sinking fund provisions have an opposite effect but the results of such market operations by the borrower are much more difficult to qualify. If the partial retirement is used, the number of bonds in existence will diminish, leaving a smaller float in the secondary market in its wake. Similarly, yields become difficult to calculate since the real end-date of these bonds can only be averaged down. But generally purchase and/or sinking funds will help to keep a bond's yield low in all but the strongest markets. It should be noted that many US corporate and foreign bonds have these provisions attached. In order to avoid an outright sinking fund (retiring bonds at par by lot), many issues have optional purchase funds enabling the borrower to purchase bonds in the open market in anticipation of sinking fund retirement day. This can only benefit the investor since it helps raise the secondary market price. A classic sinking fund will redeem his bonds from him involuntarily if his number has been drawn by lot.

Cross-hedging can be a combination of apples and oranges unless the basis is reflective of compatibility in the instruments matched. And while perfect compatibility is as unrealistic as the perfect hedge, the basis should be reduced to essential risk only if it is to have a chance of success.

FUTURES PRICING

The way in which bond and GNMAs are priced succinctly bring many of the variables already discussed in both cash and futures markets into perspective. As with the pricing of any commodity future, a multitude of factors can be brought together *ad hoc*, never to be repeated again in exactly the same manner. But the common denominator of all fixed income futures pricing is the somewhat inelegant concept of 'cheapness'; that is, the pricing mechanism of the future is the cheapest cash instrument which can be delivered against it.

A short seller faced with delivery of a cash instrument will be required to purchase a deliverable bond. Among many, one bond will be a better bargain than the others. For the longer dated bonds this issue will be, *ceteris paribus*, the most recent high coupon issue.

This pricing refers to the spot month only – the closest contract. Other futures in alternate delivery months have other factors affecting their prices, so this discussion must first discuss the pricing of the spot contract. Obviously, the cheapest bond becomes the common denominator for other futures pricing.

How is cheapness of a bond determined? Price alone, as reflected in yield, is not the single determining criterion as a superficial glance might first suggest. Without digressing into a discussion of relative value on interest-bearing instruments, the following generalisation, given what has already been said concerning cheapness, is the rule followed when considering delivery: for yield maintenance contracts, the bond with the highest yield will also be the cheapest to deliver. For principal maintenance contracts the factor must be used for this determination.

For example, consider a short seller who must deliver $1 million of long-term bonds to fulfil delivery obligations. Several bonds present themselves as candidates. Their closing prices and yields were as follows:

bond	price	yield	factor
14% of 2011 @	$123^{11}/_{32}$ = 11.22		1.6333
$12\frac{3}{4}$ of 2010 @	$113^{26}/_{32}$ = 11.13		1.4938
$13^7/_8$ of 2011 @	$122^{25}/_{32}$ = 11.20		1.6155
10 of 2010 @	$93^{25}/_{32}$ = 10.68		1.2061

If yield were the only, or most popular, criterion then the 14% would be the obvious choice. But by using the factor method, the $13^7/_8$ becomes the cheapest bond. This is determined in the following manner. The CBT close for the future was $75^{22}/_{32}$ on the same day. Using this, plus the factors indicated, the delivery amount in dollars, including accrued interest, minus the cash closing price (both expressed in either decimals or 32nds) gives in each case here a small loss. The smallest loss is in fact therefore the cheapest bond of the group to deliver.[5]

No spot price would normally be expected to be exactly the same as the cash price of the cheapest instrument. If this was so in a static sense then there would be no reason for the futures market to exist. Therefore, cheapness as a variable is the most single important component of principal maintenance contracts.

The second element of the futures pricing has to do with the forward rates rather than the spot *per se*. In the first chapter, we described the difference between spot and forward as simply the impact of the cost of money plus expectations.

While the latter is ultimately the fuel upon which a futures market runs it nevertheless is a vague concept which on many occasions cannot be quantified. But the former can obviously be quantified in the markets and also helps to put a value on the concept of normal backwardation also used in the first chapter.

The basic difference between spot and forward prices is the cost of carry; that amount of money at which one carries a position. More simply it is the rate at which one borrows money to run a security position. In the American bond market this is known as the re-po rate, short for rate at which re-purchase agreements are accomplished.[6] In the financial futures market it is known by several names, depending upon the length and nature of the instrument involved. As we shall define it here, it is expressed as follows:

$$\text{cost of carry} = \frac{\text{futures coupon}}{S} \times \frac{360}{365} + \frac{P - S}{S} \times \frac{360}{T}$$

where

S = spot price
P = nearby price
T = period between S and P

In the most simple example, the result will equal the difference between the two prices S and P.

The cost of carry has several nuances. It is very tempting to assume that as one looks over forward prices of a constant bond future, implications for future yield levels can be drawn. While this is a tantalising assumption, it is at heart incorrect. What these forward prices indicate is the bond futures market's thoughts concerning short-term rates. Another way of stating this is to say, in technical terms, that the percentage difference between forward prices is nothing more than an extension of the term re-po rate. Arranging re-pos for terms longer than perhaps one month can be difficult, but through use of the futures markets they may be extended somewhat farther than ordinarily possible in the cash market.

Forward futures prices are then nothing more than an extrapolation of short-term rates into the future. Anyone attempting to create a yield curve using them would fall into a serious trap, as the next section will show. But more importantly, they do give a quantifiable meaning to normal backwardation. When forward prices are lower than spot they reflect a downward sloping price curve. A trader's definition of this is that the next offer is lower than the previous bid. This is essentially true but in this case the reason is not necessarily a falling market but only a reflection of the cost of money over the period involved.

Many different interpretations can be implied from this condition. One could justifiably assume from it that if prices in the future only deviate from the spot by the carrying cost then, in a sense, a state of equilibrium exists, with investors not being drawn into forward contracts because of no compelling desire to do so. Or on a slightly negative note, one could also assume that prices are slumping because investor outlook is not particularly favourable for the immediate future and therefore no one is bidding strongly for certain futures months. However, in this latter case, it is eminently possible that floor traders would take advantage of any anomaly, thereby quickly correcting the entire spectrum of forward prices. Under such circumstances the basic cost of carry is still the best assumption that one can make about the future based upon futures prices.

FUTURES TIME AND YIELD CURVES

The fundamental difference between the cash yield curve and the curve represented by futures prices, or yields of any particular instrument, is one of degree rather than of time. Both are in the same dimension. The term structure of interest rates gives an indication of the cost of money for any particular maturity, while futures prices do nothing more than give one the opportunity to buy or sell at today's price up to two years in the future at a price reflective of the cost of money.

There is a strong temptation to think of that time curve as a yield curve unto itself. For instance, does it not give an indication of what investors and traders think about yield levels on the respective instrument in one or two years time? The answer is 'no'. Time curves are normally expected to show gradations in price based upon a standard variation but to read any more into them leads to serious misinterpretation. The yield curve is one-dimensional in time; that is, it is a reflection of today's market reaction. The futures time curve is also one-dimensional in that it reflects only a small part of the overall yield curve. It certainly is not a time machine, spanning the divide between present and future.

The same is true of the futures yield curve. In order to construct one, the closing prices on Treasury bills, ten-year notes and long bond contracts would be required. Obviously this would not be a complete curve and will do nothing more than reflect the cash curve for the same maturities, less basis. No matter how one adjusts time or yield curves, they still reflect the present cash markets.

What role then do expectations play in futures pricing and yields? Surely they cannot be totally relegated to the proverbial dustbin in favour of purely mechanical considerations. While this is certainly true it must be added that it is difficult to quantify. Consider the situation where the time curve swings from a downward slope to an upward slope. Is this an indication of investors believing that rates will turn down in the future and locking in today's yields to the extent that prices uniformly rise? Perhaps, but more probable is the fact that short-term interest rates have changed. If any investors did adopt this tactic, very few non-professionals would even actually recognise the ploy.

An example here will illustrate both an investor's desires and a trader's reactions. This cannot fully cover the range of trading reactions that could potentially occur but does cover the general ground.

Suppose that a corporate borrower, on the best advice, believes that long-term bond rates will begin to move up in two weeks' time. In about that time the borrower has a new long-term borrowing planned and would certainly like to lock in today's rate before the imminent rise. This new issue is planned for $100 million so every ¹/₈% rise in rates could cost him a potential $125 000.

Assume that $100 million worth of long bond contracts are sold short, ignoring a partial hedge for the moment. The contract sold is not the spot (terminating in three weeks) but the nearby. This is done so as not to close the contract position prematurely in case the borrower wants to keep the short open even longer. The selling pressure of this large number of contracts pushes the nearby price down by ¼ point (we assume that he can in fact short this large amount in the respective contract month). The results before and after this operation, assuming there are no other price aberrations, can be seen in Figure 4.2.

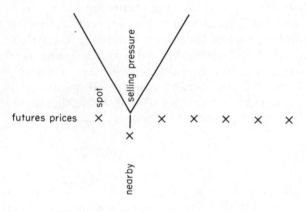

FIGURE 4.2 Short-selling Effect

As the borrower sells, the contract price will move out of line with the spot and other nearby months. But it should not be assumed that the price will close the day at this depressed level. Many floor traders may have spread positions involving this delivery month and will quickly readjust their positions as they see this large order on the exchange floor. Therefore, the depressed price may have a ripple effect in surrounding delivery months. Or, on the other hand, the depressed price may attract other traders who believe the contract is too cheap and who now will begin buying to take advantage of the price anomaly.

In two weeks' time, assume that the presumption was correct and bonds have fallen by $\frac{1}{4}$ point in price. The potential borrower adds this trading profit to his increased cost of borrowing, thereby helping to offset increased costs.[7] As his contract position is closed, the opposite of the original process now occurs and that particular contract rises in price. But the buying pressure is not now a sign of optimism about rates but simply a matter of short covering, which has a momentary effect at best. And again, floor traders may have to unwind positions just as they did in the original case.

Anyone able to observe this activity purely through price quotations would have a difficult time ascertaining the underlying movements here. Added to this is the fact that some forward prices are not representative of investor activity and may be marked to market only, reflecting a lack of liquidity. A rule of thumb on bond futures is also true of many others: the farther in time the forward price is from the spot the less liquidity the contract will have. Generally, only the spot and the two closest months will generate any real liquidity although it is still possible to trade the more distant months, with somewhat less efficiency.

NOTES

1. The one exception to this is the category of low coupon Treasury bonds issued in the early 1950s through late 1960s known as 'flower bonds'. These obligations bear low coupons and are issued at a discount. Upon the death of the beneficial owner, they can be redeemed at par, the capital gain not being subject to tax.
2. Treasury bills are quoted on a discount basis while bonds are quoted on a coupon yield basis. Therefore an adjustment must be made in order to provide a comparable yield calculation. This is referred to as a coupon equivalent basis and is applied to T-bills so that they may be stated in bond terms. It is as follows:

$$\text{coupon equivalent} = \frac{365 \times \text{discount}}{360 - (\text{discount} \times \text{time})}$$

3. This has the effect of raising yield. The yield on a GNMA is

then necessarily adjusted upward if stated in semi-annual terms.

4. In order to arrive at a suitable fifteen-year maturity the end date on the deliverable bond must be that length after rounding down its life to the nearest quarter (of a year), starting from the first day of the delivery month.

5. This calculation is based upon 30 December 1982 and 12 December 1982 delivery dates. Although the example simplifies the process by not specifically mentioning accrued interest, it should be noted that all the bonds used in this example pay interest in May and November.

6. A repurchase agreement, or re-po, works as follows. A holder of Treasury securities agrees to sell a holding to another, usually a dealer, and agrees to buy them back after a short period of time at a slightly higher price. The higher price is the rate in federal funds for the period involved. This commonly used method is actually a short-term loan made by one dealer to another, using the securities involved as collateral.

7. The amount of profit made in this example would save the borrower only $\frac{1}{4}$% interest on his first year interest bill. Otherwise he would pay the increased $\frac{1}{4}$% throughout the remaining life of the loan.

5 Innovations in Futures Markets

The development of a futures market is a risky enterprise. Before the market starts trading, capital must be injected into constructing the market-place, and into marketing, research and development. In the market's early days of existence, trading members are likely to suffer an income-loss compared with what they would have earned elsewhere, even before a deduction is made for the cost of capital injected to date. If the market is fortunate enough to enter a self-supporting period, where members make high returns both to the financial and human capital they have invested in the market-place, the future is far from assured. Today's successful contract can become tomorrow's failure. Continual research into new contract forms and experimentation are essential to maintaining market success. Nor must the exchange itself develop into an oligarchy jealously protecting its privileges but it must show a dynamic approach to membership expansion.

DEVELOPING THE MARKET-PLACE

Chicago's Mercantile Exchange (CME) took the innovatory step in 1972 of launching the world's first financial futures exchange – the International Monetary Market (IMM). The first contracts to be launched were in currencies. Then a gold contract followed in December 1974. The ninety-day T-bill contract was introduced in January 1976. Then there was a

141

pause in innovative activity, with the next major step being the introduction of a CD futures contract in 1981.

The IMM began as a separate corporation in partnership with the CME. Until 1972 the CME had concentrated on trading futures for agricultural products – cattle, pigs, pork bellies, plywood, and lumber for example. The IMM was set up to trade financial futures. At its inception the IMM issued 650 memberships. Seats were offered to CME members at a token $100 each, while the public could buy them at $10 000 each. The sums raised through seat issue went towards pre-opening capital expenditure. Given that the IMM started operations on only a small part of the already existing CME trading floor, initial capital costs were well contained. It was not until many years later, as trading expanded, that the IMM came to be allotted substantial space including trading pits. Many of the members of the IMM were active also on the other CME markets, and so if trading was light on the IMM they could step over to one of the traditional markets. Thus the physical integration of the IMM with the other CME markets helped to reduce the potential opportunity cost which IMM members had to set against their IMM earnings in the early days of operations.

The proximity of the IMM and CME trading was helpful to the development of financial futures trading in other respects. Members of CME who were also IMM members had an incentive to interest their traditional commodity customers in the new financial futures markets. Such customers were fertile ground for business development, as they were already well accustomed to the methods of dealing in futures markets, and the marketing costs were small of promoting to them the benefits of futures trading. The CME member himself, or his floor broker, could fulfil the customer's orders on the IMM section of the floor as well as in the commodity pits. The importance of complementary business has been particularly noticeable in Canadian dollars, where as much as 50 per cent of business emanates from corporations active in lumber, plywood or grains.

As on other US futures exchanges, memberships of the IMM are sold to individuals, not to corporations. A membership gives the holder the right to trade on the floor of the exchange. Only the owner, his agent, or his tenant, where a lease arrangement exists, can trade. Where a large firm of commission brokers, for example, wishes to have several of their staff trading on the floor, it must buy in the name of individuals an equal number of memberships, perhaps entering into lease arrangements with some individual employees.

The individual subscription for memberships on US exchanges contrasts sharply with the corporate subscription that characterises UK exchanges. There memberships are sold to companies (or partnerships) who are entitled to have a given number of their employees trade on the floor. Thus in UK exchanges seats are priced at a level that reflects the potential earning power of several traders; an individual who does not wish to form an organisation and employ several traders would usually be deterred by the price of a seat bid to a level that reflected its benefit to large firms. Thus the British membership structure discourages the lone or independent trader. Yet it is likely that the 'local' – the well-capitalised individual trader – operating his own undertaking has greater incentive towards efficiency than the employee of the larger organisation.

Indeed, in US exchanges experience shows that often the more able traders employed by the big organisations decide that there are greater rewards from being independent and buy their own seats. Many of the traders in US futures exchanges are in their third generation; already their grandfather held a seat, and the trading skills have been passed on. Individual memberships are conducive to the small business being able to obtain an important market share in the futures industry. The success of independents in holding market share is not due to any implicit subsidy, but presumably to comparative advantage in certain dealing functions, particularly scalping. In contrast, the British system of membership puts a handicap in the way of the small trader.

IMM memberships may be transferred by an open market transaction between the present and future owner. The price of IMM memberships has displayed substantial volatility albeit against a rising trend. From an issue price of $10 000 in 1972, prices of over $200 000 were realised in the years 1979–80. Some price retreat was evident in 1981–2. The price of a seat reflects the present value of the net rental income which a marginal purchaser would expect to earn in the years ahead; rental income is defined as the difference between the net income which the member makes from his being able to trade on the floor and the opportunity cost of the time which he spends there (where the opportunity cost is taken as the alternative earnings which he could make in the same time elsewhere).

The income which the member derives from being physically present on the floor may come from several sources. He may act as a floor broker, executing orders for outsiders, and earning commission income thereon. Alternatively, from his vantage point on the floor he can observe the periodic ebb and flow of orders and act profitably as a scalper. Having immediate access to information and being able to deal immediately on the floor, he should profit from less well-placed customers. Lastly, there may be scope for profit from the collusive-type activities on which commodity futures market regulators frown.

If seat prices rose to very high levels, this may be taken as *prima facie* evidence of restrictive practices or the exercise of market power by the IMM; in these circumstances an expansion of the number of members which would bring downward pressure on charges (implicit or explicit) could be justified on traditional anti-trust arguments. A substantial price for a seat is not in itself, however, convincing proof that the trading public is being exploited; the capital intensity of the market and the risks incurred in its development must also be assessed.

Seat-holders are in effect equity-holders in the exchange. The original holders supply the initial capital out of which the pre-opening marketing and development costs, and the capital costs of providing the trading area, are paid; the initial capital is applied also to furnishing the Exchange with liquid assets. In addition, the initial members furnish capital implicitly to the extent of earning loss (compared to what they could have earned elsewhere) during the early stages of operation. The aggregate value of seats would have to exceed the capital invested in the exchange before there was even any question of investigating whether seat prices were 'excessive'.

Furthermore, some capital gain on the price of a seat should be viewed as a return to risk. When the original members sunk capital into the exchange they took a risk that all could be lost and the venture prove a failure. The chance of a substantial capital gain being realised is essential to the attraction of capital for setting up an exchange.

The number of seats in an exchange does not have to remain constant for evermore. The present membership can agree collectively (according to a procedure laid down by the exchange's constitution) to issue new seats. The normal method by which new seats would be created is by rights issue; existing members would obtain the right to a new seat or a given fraction of a new seat and these could be sold in an open market. An individual member would vote in favour of a given proposed expansion in the number of members if he believed that any loss of trading income, which he would suffer due to the increased competition for business, would be more than compensated for by the net sale proceeds he obtained on the rights issue, less any capital loss on his existing seat (due to an increased availability of seats).

Several factors could dispose the member favourably towards an expansion of the number of seats. He may believe that a shortage of dealing manpower on the floor is causing customers' orders to be fulfilled inefficiently. If the number of dealers were increased and gains in efficiency realised, then business may be extended to such an extent as to mean little loss of revenue to existing members. It may be that there is considerable business potential in trading new contracts, and that such business would be complementary to that already being conducted, yet an expansion of dealing capacity would be needed to cope with the increased volume. An example of complementary business is the trading of currency and interest-rate futures; many of the trading public who become accustomed to covering interest-rate risks on the IMM are readily convinced of the advantages of also placing some of their currency business there.

Particular interests in membership expansion can diverge. The commission broking firm which holds several memberships (these are held indirectly through named individuals) and whose earnings are derived mainly out of commissions paid by the trading public would be well disposed to a membership expansion promising increased turnover. The local independent, who acts as a scalper or floor broker and is already stretched to his capacity limit, is likely to be less favourably disposed towards membership expansion which is likely to promise pressure on his profit margins.

Despite the lack of unanimity with respect to the issue of membership expansion, the IMM, together with the Chicago Mercantile Exchange, have succeeded in increasing their numbers. In 1981, after a series of meetings involving members from all areas of the exchange, a new Membership Rights Programme was submitted to the membership and approved overwhelmingly. The programme provided for an eventual 25 per cent increase in membership. Membership has also been increased directly through the issue of seats for which the holders are restricted to trading on subsidiaries or associates of the CME. It has already been discussed how seats on the IMM, an associate market of the CME, were issued. In April 1982, a new division of the CME was created – the Index and Option Market (IOM). During 1981 it became apparent that the CME would soon receive approval by the Commodity Futures Trading Commission (CFTC) to list the S&P 500 Stock Index contract and at least one options contract. This made an expansion of dealing capacity essential. Hence the new IOM was launched. One thousand memberships of the new division were sold to present CME and IMM members; in addition 200 memberships were sold to people or institutions with experience in securities or options trading. The combination of the expansion programmes in 1981 and 1982 would bring total Exchange membership to more than 2500, about double what it had been during the 1970s.

We have already referred to members in an Exchange being in the position of equity-holders. The Chicago Mercantile Exchange earns income from a variety of sources, prominent among which are clearance fees (levied on each transaction), interest income (earned on the liquid assets held by the exchange), and quotation data fees (levied on members to contribute towards the cost of providing continuous quotation on display boards and on Reuter systems). Balance sheet and income statements are summarised in Tables 5.1 and 5.2 below.

TABLE 5.1   Chicago Mercantile Exchange Balance Sheets
(31 December 1981 and 1980)

Assets	1981	1980
Cash	691 488	126 452
Short-term investments	3 572 466	2 919 359
Accounts receivable	1 606 573	1 877 772
Investment in CME		
Centre Partnership	888 889	—
Property, net of accumulated		
depreciation and amortisation	16 909 899	16 977 650
Other assets	798 230	373 062
	$24 467 545	$22 274 295
Liabilities		
Accounts payable and		
accrued expenses	5 612 050	4 521 767
Payable to Chicago		
Mercantile Trust	4 710 961	4 342 500
Members' equity	14 144 534	13 410 028
	$24 467 545	$22 274 295

In the balance sheet, the principal assets are the property, in which the CME markets are located, and short-term investments. These assets have been funded principally out of initial membership contributions plus accumulated earnings. In the income statement, expenses relate to salaries of exchange officials (including those on the floor and in general administration), to public relations and promotion, and to property occupancy. It can be seen that public relations and promotion are a significant component of overall expense. Many traders admit that the CME has been one of Chicago's well-run political machines, with public relations in Washington having played an important part in gaining the official approvals vital to trading expansion.

TABLE 5.2 Chicago Mercantile Exchange Income Statement

Income	1981	1980
Clearance fees	$21 494 563	$19 980 257
Interest income	5 764 739	4 380 603
Quotation data fees	2 365 426	702 793
Fines	496 261	417 951
Membership dues	64 752	65 000
Other operating income	996 336	869 060
Total income	$31 182 077	$26 415 664
Expenses		
Salaries and employee benefits	$11 088 991	$8 809 671
General and administrative	7 114 267	6 213 501
Public relations and promotion	5 076 572	4 378 204
Occupancy	2 779 817	2 475 670
Contributions to Chicago Mercantile Trust	3 959 924	4 342 500
Total expenses	$30 019 571	$26 219 546
Income before taxes	$1 162 506	$196 118
Provision for taxes	428 000	50 000
Net income	$734 506	$146 118
Members' equity, at beginning of year	13 410 028	13 263 910
Members' equity, at end of year	$14 144 534	$13 410 028

The CME (including the IMM and IOM) does not have a monopoly in financial futures trading in Chicago. The Chicago Board of Trade (CBT), the centre of grain futures trading in the USA, houses active markets in US bond futures. Indeed, the Board of Trade had by the early 1980s won prime position in bond futures, with its GNMA, T-bond, and T-note contracts having become industry leaders. The IMM's experiment with a short-term Treasury note contract had proved a failure. The Board of Trade's attempt to compete, however, with the CME in short-term interest-rate contracts proved unsuccessful. Its commercial paper contract failed for reasons already discussed in Chapter 3; then in 1982, after one year of trying to compete with the IMM in trading a new CD futures contract, defeat was acknowledged. The IMM's early success in promoting the T-bill futures gave it a position of considerable advantage in promoting new short-term interest-rate contracts. Locals in the IMM could engage in spread trading between the T-bill futures market and the new CD futures contract, and this provided liquidity in the early stages of the new market. On the Board of Trade, locals did not see many trading opportunities in the new contract, and did not give it much attention.

The Board of Trade failed to make its entry into the stock index futures market in mid-1982, when both the CME and New York's Financial Futures Exchange (NYFFE) launched stock index contracts. The Board of Trade's setback was due to its having designed a contract based on the Dow Jones index and then encountering legal opposition from Dow Jones Inc. to the use of its index in futures trading. Chicago critics pointed to this as an example of the Board of Trade's lack of political muscle or research effort. A lack of common purpose among Board of Trade members, with divisions often running along ethnic boundaries, was held responsible.

The London International Financial Futures Exchange (LIFFE) had a more ambitious opening than the IMM. Rather than starting its trading life on simply a small section of an existing commodity market floor, LIFFE was born into a grand building refurbished at considerable expense. The capacity of the Royal Exchange building was sufficient to handle the trading volume which it took the IMM ten years to build up. The high front-end costs of the London market were reflected in the high issue price of seats (£30 000 to outsiders, £20 000 to a first round of members whose inclusion was considered promotional to the new market) and high running costs.

LIFFE followed the practice of other British exchanges of issuing corporate memberships and so discouraging the participation of 'locals'. The insulation of the LIFFE market-place from the other London commodity markets was a handicap to the early promotion of business. Floor traders in LIFFE, unlike in the IMM during its early days, did not have the opportunity during slack periods to simply move over to one of the other trading pits. Nor could floor brokers in the new market act also as floor brokers in the older established markets. Arbitrage transactions between the commodity and interest-rate futures markets, as described in Chapter 3, can often be effected on the same floor in the Chicago Mercantile Exchange, but not in London.

According to industry estimates in Chicago, around 75% of the outside public trading on the IMM is speculative. There is a long history in the USA of wealthy individuals trading speculatively on futures markets. In Britain the market of wealthy individuals is smaller than in the USA and there is no tradition of futures speculation. Thus LIFFE was faced with an uphill marketing struggle. To develop speculative business of similar proportions to Chicago, an international marketing effort would almost certainly be needed. Clients from Benelux, France, Germany and Switzerland would have to be won. Many brokers are reticent to accept German business due to the treatment of futures trading as gaming under German law, making the collection of debts unenforceable.

STOCK INDEX FUTURES

The most spontaneously successful contract introduced into US financial futures markets has been that for stock indices. In mid-1982 the Kansas futures market started stock index futures trading and was quickly followed by the IMM and NYFFE. Within several weeks the latter two markets were already trading daily volumes of around 50 000 and 25 000 respectively. Before analysing the reasons for the rapid take-off of the stock contracts, let us first take a look at the contracts in detail.

The IMM's contract is based on the S&P 500 Stock Index. This is based on the equity prices of 500 different companies – 400 industrials, 40 utilities, 20 transportation companies and 40 financial institutions. The market value of the 500 firms is equal to approximately 80% of the value of all stocks listed on the New York Stock Exchange. Each stock in the index receives a weight equal to the share of the issuing corporation's total equity value in the combined equity market value of the 500 firms. In technical language, the S&P index is a market-weighted index. The index is calculated using the base years 1941–3 = 10. An index value of 150 should be interpreted as meaning that the market value of the 500 firms is 15 times greater than the base value of the index in 1941–3.

The size of the IMM contract is 500 times the value of the S&P 500 Stock Index, meaning that the contract's size would have varied between $30 000 and $100 000 over the past decade. There is no physical delivery and contracts still standing at the finish of the last day of trading are closed by cash settlement, with the difference between the previous day's closing price and the precise level of the S&P Index at 3.00 p.m. Central time on the last day of trading multiplied by 100 being payable to and receivable from the two parties to each contract. The months traded are the same as for other financial futures contracts on the IMM.

The stock futures contract traded by the New York Financial Futures Exchange is based on the NYSE Composite Index. The Composite Index is an average of the price of all the common stocks listed and traded on the New York Stock Exchange, where each corporation receives a weight according to the proportion which its market value represents in the total market value of all corporations whose shares are listed. The size of the NYFFE contract is 500 times the value of the NYSE Composite Index. It is thereby somewhat smaller in size than the IMM contract, given that the NYSE index is smaller than the S&P 500 index. On NYFFE, as on the IMM, stock index futures contracts are traded for delivery months March, June, September and December respectively. Cash settlement is based on the difference between the settlement price on the next to last day of trading and the value of the NYSE Composite Index at the close of trading of the New York Stock Exchange on the last day of trading.

Stock index futures differ from other financial futures contracts in the important respect that no simple arbitrage is possible between it and the cash markets. In principle, two-way arbitrage between say, the S&P 500 contract on the IMM, and the cash market in equities, would require the IMM trader to take a position in all 500 shares to match his position in the futures market. Transacting in 500 stocks would not only be expensive but also impossible to achieve over a very short period of time. Even if the trader could match his futures position with a position in the cash markets the arbitrage would not be riskless. For example, suppose in March 1983 the trader goes short in the S&P index futures for June delivery and simultaneously borrows dollars to purchase the 500 components of the index in the cash market. What dividend will be received from the shares is uncertain and so arbitrage profit is not riskless. Arbitrage in the direction of buying S&P futures and taking a short position in the cash market – a strategy that would look attractive when there has been heavy selling in the futures relative to in the cash market – would be especially difficult to arrange, due to the cumbersome and costly procedures involved in taking short positions in stocks.

There are certain mutual funds designed to move very closely with the S&P 500 index. These provide a channel for arbitrage between the futures and cash markets in stocks. But arbitrage pressures may in part move the price of the mutual funds relative to their net asset value rather than bringing cash and futures prices fully into alignment. In practice, the principal type of arbitrage between the cash and futures markets in stock is one-way arbitrage by investment institutions.

As an example of one-way arbitrage, consider an investment institution which holds a portfolio of equities very close in composition to the S&P 500 index. Each month the institution builds up its portfolio. The advent of the stock futures market has presented the institution with the choice, each month, of whether to make its acquisition in the futures or cash market. For example, suppose we are in March 1983, and the fund manager is considering whether to buy equities in the cash market or to buy S&P futures for June. If the premium of the futures over the present level of the index, expressed at an annual rate, is less than the three-month interest rate minus the expected dividend yield of an S&P portfolio (over the next three months), then it would appear profitable to buy S&P futures and invest the cash scheduled for equity investment into three-month money-market paper, with the intention of making cash purchases of equities in June simultaneous with the maturing of the futures contract. At the maturity, the fund manager cannot be sure of purchasing stocks at an average price equal to the settlement price of the futures contract (set as equal to the S&P index at 3.00 p.m.), because of having to allow time during which the cash transactions can be effected. Thus if a steep rise occurs in the market after 3 o'clock, the manager may lose through having postponed his purchases and bought stock futures rather than equities originally in March, despite the promising arbitrage calculation at that date.

One-way arbitrage opportunity may also be present for the fund manager who has decided to switch some of his holding of the market portfolio into cash. Suppose this decision is taken in March and the premium of the S&P futures June rate over the present level of the S&P index is greater than the three-month interest rate minus the expected dividend yield. Then it would appear profitable to delay selling the equities in the cash market and instead to sell S&P futures for June. Again, the one-way arbitrage transaction described is not riskless. In addition to the uncertainty as to the level of dividend income, there is the uncertain amount by which the manager's average sale price would differ from the S&P index whenever effected.

The various handicaps to arbitrage mean that stock index futures prices enjoy some independence from the cash market, although this freedom decreases the closer the futures contract is to maturity; at maturity the futures price equals the then value of the S&P index, by contract definition. Thus the short-term speculator in the stock index futures markets, who intends to trade in and out over a period of say one week, must take a view on more than how the S&P index will move, but also on how the futures price is likely to move relative to the index. Similarly the hedger who takes a short position in an S&P futures contract to set against his holding of a diversified equity portfolio is subject to significant basis risk if the intended duration of the hedged position is much shorter than the maturity of the futures contract.

Despite the difficulties of arbitrage between cash and futures markets, stock index futures markets quickly achieved a high level of liquidity. The success must be attributed to the popularity of the contract with investors and hedgers. A long position in stock index futures offers the small investor a degree of risk diversification that would be attainable only at very heavy cost in the cash market. The small investor can obtain diversification in the cash market through the purchase of mutual funds, but these have considerable front-end fees. Only if he intends to hold a long position in the market portfolio over a prolonged period of time would the cumulative transaction costs of rolling over positions in stock futures be greater than the front-end fees of purchasing a mutual fund plus its running management costs.

Even the large fund can gain transactions cost advantage from the use of stock index futures. For suppose the fund manager believes that a particular stock has an expected return over the next three months that is abnormally high relative to its market risk, and therefore decides to reduce slightly his holding in the market portfolio and increase that in the individual stock. To make a slight adjustment in his holding of each component of the market index as balance to the increased holding of the individual stock would be expensive in terms of transaction costs, and it would not be possible to effect all the individual transactions simul-taneously, causing his portfolio to become distorted in a random fashion during the period necessary to effect the transactions. Thus taking a short position in a stock index futures and using spare cash to buy the individual stock would appear an attractive alternative strategy, so long as stock index futures prices and the value of his standard market portfolio are highly correlated over the period in question. Early evidence on stock futures prices does suggest that there should be a high, albeit less than perfect, correlation.

Note that the fund manager is unlikely to take a short position in stock index futures to exactly the same total value as the purchase of the particular stock. Instead he is likely to choose a 'hedge-ratio' which depends on the degree of the particular stock's market risk. For example, if the stock is in a corporation whose profits are highly dependent on the stage in the business cycle, and whose price therefore tends to swing with a wider amplitude than that of the average market portfolio (in technical jargon, the stock has a Beta-coefficient greater than one), the manager could sell stock index futures to a greater value than the stock purchased. In practice Beta-coefficients cannot be measured with great precision.

Stock index futures also have an appeal to the large investor who wishes to trade on a view as to how the market index will move over a short period of time. For example, suppose a large investor intends to trade on a view about the market's movement over the next week. If he were to buy a portfolio in the cash market by effecting many individual deals, with the intention of dealing similarly on disposal, he would be subject to the risk that the average purchase and sale prices would be significantly different from the index level at each time. Where the speculation is over a short period, divergences between the average dealing price and the market index may account for a large share of the potential speculative profit. The appeal of stock index futures to the short-term speculator causes their price performance to be somewhat more volatile than that of the underlying market. The short-term traders are generally more influenced than are those longer term traders in the cash markets by technical analysis of price movements (often called chartism) to the exclusion of fundamental analysis.

Speculators are likely to be more common on the long than on the short side of the stock index futures market. This supposition follows from some widely accepted premises of portfolio analysis. In particular, a diversified equity market portfolio is assumed to be priced in the capital markets at a level such as to offer the average investor an expected return superior to that obtainable on low or zero risk securities (for example, Treasury bills). The investor whose views about market prospects were close to the mainstream would not go short in the market portfolio, for this would represent a higher risk position than one which contained only Treasury bills, and yet the expected return would be lower (given that the expected return on equities is higher than on cash).

Indeed, only the speculator, whose expectation of returns from the market portfolio was inferior to the average market participant's expectation by more than the normal risk premium on the market portfolio, should consider taking an outright short position in stock futures with no offsetting holding of stocks in the cash market-place. Thus short-sellers of stock index futures are most likely to be hedgers – individuals or corporations who are using the futures market as a vehicle for reducing their net long position in the stock market.

Some corporations and individuals may use the stock index futures market to cover their economic exposure to the risk of stock market fluctuations. For example, a firm of stock-brokers may find that its business volume and profitability is positively correlated with the level of the stock index; it can hedge fluctuations in profitability by taking a short position in stock futures. A firm of accountants specialising in liquidation work would find that its profits rose during recession and fell during boom; the firm could hedge profit fluctuations by taking a long position in stock index futures. Hedging is not costless; the cumulative brokerage costs – explicit and implicit – of rolling over futures contracts as they mature are incurred. The more able are the owners of the stockbroking firm, or of the accounting firm, to absorb risk (usually due to their having large wealth-holding outside the given business) the less ready will they be to spend resources on insurance (equivalently, the less willing will they be to incur the brokerage costs of rolling over futures contracts).

Stock index futures have a hedging potential for the small businessman. For example, consider the entrepreneur whose business represents a large share of his total wealth, and which is in a highly cyclical sector of the economy (e.g. house building). He can reduce the risk of his overall portfolio (including business and non-business assets) by having the corporation which he controls take a short position in stock index futures. Thus, if the economy fell unexpectedly into recession, the corporation would make a profit from its short position in stock futures, and this would offset to some extent the fall in profitability of the underlying business activity. Moreover, by taking a short position in stock index futures, the corporation should improve the credit ranking given by its bank, as the volatility of its earnings and the risk of bankruptcy are reduced. In effect, by his corporation taking a short position in stock index futures, the businessman in a cyclical industry can obtain some of the benefits of personal risk reduction and availability of bank finance that could be obtained from a public issue of equity. Even if the corporation were just large enough to consider making a public issue of shares, the costs of this are high and would be likely to compare unfavourably with rolling over short positions in futures; comparison would be especially unfavourable where the entrepreneur is unsure of how long he will hold the present business, and so his risk exposure may be of fairly short duration.

The stock index futures contract has proved useful to businesses active in the stock market itself. Specialists on the New York Stock Exchange (specialists perform a market-making function) often find that they have net holdings of stocks overnight; the risk of these can be covered, albeit imperfectly, by taking a short position in stock index futures. The fifteen minutes later closing time of the Chicago stock index futures market to that of the New York Stock Exchange provides important flexibility to specialists. Often the specialist needs a small amount of time after the close of the NYSE to calculate precisely his inventory position. In choosing the hedge ratio (the number of contracts to offset against his inventory position), the specialist should be aware of his inventory's Beta-coefficient (see p. 155). If the Beta is high, a high hedge-ratio would be required; if Beta is near zero – indicating that the price of the stocks held has zero correlation with the stock market index – then stock futures would be of no use as a hedge.

The underwriter, like the specialist, can use stock index futures to reduce risk. By taking a short position in futures the underwriter can hedge himself against a loss realised on the new issue of shares due to a general decline in the stock market. Again the chosen hedge-ratio should depend on the estimated Beta of the stocks being issued. If the Beta-coefficient is low, stock index futures would not offer much possibility for reducing risk exposure.

INTEREST-RATE OPTIONS

Options on fixed interest instruments differ substantially in concept and structure from interest-rate futures, although their functions are the same. Because of this difference they also afford hedgers and speculators a different sort of risk environment although reward ratios differ only slightly from futures markets. At the time of writing, bond and money-market options are still in their nascent stage and their practical success has yet to be proven. We will therefore concentrate upon their general characteristics and uses.

Interest-rate options are initially to be traded on the options rather than on the commodity exchanges. Their developmental history will be somewhat different from futures in that they will be traded by people, in some cases, more accustomed to trading listed options. Since they will follow a different model their language will be somewhat different from futures patois.

By their very name, options suggest vehicles which may or may not be exercised, depending upon the holder's prerogative. This is a fundamental of options at variance with futures which must be mandatorily closed unless delivery is required. While options present the same type of leverage as futures, they therefore possess a different sort of risk structure.

Options settle in the cash instrument upon which they are based. Unlike some futures, they can be denominated in small contracts aimed at the small investor. They should, however, be distinguished from options on futures contracts, a rather specialised market discussed in the next section.

There are two types of option, regardless of whether we are discussing fixed income instruments or shares. These are called 'calls' and 'puts'. The former is an option to buy, enabling its owner to buy a stock at a predetermined price for a specified period while the latter is an option to sell. Both sorts have a specific termination date and a series. Normally, they expire at a given date in every third month of a quarterly series. The average interest-rate option will probably be similar to the existing share options in that it will be issued for no longer than nine months into the future.

Currently, interest-rate options are confined to the American and Dutch options markets. The Chicago Board Options Exchange (CBOE) and the American Stock Exchange (AMEX) trade, or plan to trade, options on T-bills, CDs, T-bonds, and GNMAs. The Amsterdam options exchange trades options on Dutch government bonds. Although the differences between them are centred around deliverable instruments, this description will be confined to generalities about the American market.

As a right to buy, a call may be originated by a seller (writer) or a buyer. A writer is a person who decides to sell a call against a cash position he is holding. This is referred to as 'covered' writing in that the investor holds the securities he could have called from him. There is also another sort of call selling called 'naked' or uncovered writing whereby the seller is short of a physical, having no cash position in hand with which to cover. In either case, the purchaser buys a right to buy, making him the ultimate exerciser in this process.

Uncovered writing may not be necessary if a similar short-selling strategy using puts is employed. This method arose on the share options exchanges only after calls had been in existence for several years. Puts were introduced sometime thereafter. Now that the option to sell is in more general use naked call writing will probably diminish in popularity.

As an option to sell, a put purchased by one wary of a market's strength is tantamount to short selling. The person purchasing it buys the right to 'put' it to the seller at the striking price. In weak markets the price of the put will appreciate as its underlying security weakens in price. The seller assumes this risk for the premium he received by selling in the first instance.

The price at which an option may be exercised is referred to as the 'striking' price. This level is set in advance by the exchange involved and depends upon the market price of the stock at the time. A bond option, issued at 100 to reflect the underlying bond at par, may subsequently have other strike prices issued at say 98 and 102 to reflect cash market price movements. A deliverable bond standing at 102 in the cash market with options at 100 and 102 will have a higher premium attached to the 100 series than to the 102 series.

Price tiering of this nature can ultimately lead to many forms of arbitrage; sometimes more than that witnessed in the futures market where cash and futures prices move in tandem, given a basis differential. As a cash instrument vacillates in price and as more option strike prices are issued, the list of open contract prices and delivery months becomes clustered. Striking prices below the current cash price are referred to as 'out-of-the-money' options while those above the strike are referred to as 'in-the-money', regardless of the actual premium attached to them.

Arbitrage can thus occur between options of different strike prices, in different delivery months, or between different options. A bewildering array can present itself, especially if the underlying stock has been particularly price active. Traders will be able to adopt many of the same views held in the futures markets with one fundamental difference; the risk they incur is limited to the amount initially paid for the particular option series.

In the futures markets, price reflects cash market price but by the very nature of the futures contracts exposes the trader to the full effects of cash market movements. If a cash price moves ten or fifteen full points, the investor either gains or loses to the full extent of the movement. If the position is closed, the full gain or loss is realised. In the options markets the total risk is limited to the premium paid for the option. No other risk is attached. The only other option strategies which are more risky, exposing the investor to a chance of increased risk, are the uncovered positions a trader/investor may assume. In any event, this worst case example assumes that the position is left open to a call and not closed out before expiration. The overwhelming majority of options, as their futures counterparts, are closed out before expiration. This does not exclude calls which can be made during the life of a call for highly technical reasons.

For this reason, options can be said to offer perhaps as much leverage or gearing potential as a futures contract, but this depends upon the actual price paid for the position. Not all options will offer as much volatility as the spot or nearby month of a futures contract. This sort of price sensitivity is usually reserved for in-the-money calls with hefty price premiums. Because of these levels, traders tend to be less passive with their money than if they were occupied with an out-of-the-money option.

The following example illustrates this. A Treasury bond call contract is quoted for the spot month at four different striking prices. Assume the underlying bond closed at 97 and the spot month striking prices are at 93, 95, 97 and 99. This would give them respective nominal prices in two series only; the 93 and 95 series would have to be worth at least 4 and 2 (% of par of the contract size) nominal value. Added to this will be a premium, depending upon the market's expectations plus the cost of carry. Assume that the total premiums are $4\frac{1}{4}$ and $2\frac{1}{2}$.[1]

The two out-of-the-money calls are priced at say $\frac{7}{8}$ for the 97 and $\frac{3}{4}$ for the 99. The amount of leverage provided by these options is quite distinct. On a \$100 000 bond option contract one could pay as little as \$750 ($\frac{3}{4}$ of 1 %) or as much as \$4250 (4.25%). It therefore becomes rather obvious why the in-the-money 93 will be more volatile than the others. As its futures market counterpart, its price movement should be extremely price sensitive.

Options, unlike futures, use a simpler method of determining deliverable grades of cash securities. Treasury bond options represent a single cash instrument. Calculations such as those outlined in Chapter 4 are not necessary, although some may feel this is a limiting factor since a single bond may not be indicative of the entire market. Treasury bill, CD, and GNMA options use a different sort of simple method to determine deliverable grade. The two money-market instruments use a strict calendar basis to ensure that eligible instruments have a proper term to maturity. The GNMA option almost by default is still the most difficult, using a yield maintenance basis to determine which instruments in the cash market may satisfy delivery. However, there is no principal maintenance method employed here.

Of the myriad strategies involving options, several of the more simple types illustrate their advantages to investors and traders. The first two are used to augment the income on a fixed income instrument and are particularly advantageous for those seeking high income, while the others are basic forms of spreading to take limited advantage of interest-rate movements.

A covered call writer holding Treasury bonds can use options to augment the bonds' yield. If a bond yielded 11% and was also represented by an option, the holder could sell calls against the cash position, adding the premium/s received to his total return. The striking price he chooses to write at, and the amount subsequently received, will reflect the risk he assumes of having his bonds called away from him.

Conversely, an investor who wanted to protect his holdings against capital loss could use puts as a short hedge by buying a put against his position. If the bond were to depreciate in value because of an interest-rate rise, then the put would gain in value and compensate the investor when eventually closed out. The price paid on the put will, however, reduce the total return on the bond's interest payments.

As with futures, the simpler uses of options seem fairly straightforward when compared with the more complex spreading strategies. The two most popular forms of spreads are bull and bear spreads, dependent upon the investor's perception of future market movements. A bull spread is simply based upon the view that rates will fall and call prices increase. The trader then buys the lower of two call striking prices and sells the higher; the spread between them has been locked in and is his ultimate risk. If rates perform as expected, the lower strike price will move to a stronger premium and the higher level call will also appreciate. The spread will then be closed out with a large gain on the lower level call and a small loss on the higher. The reason for doing this rather than simply buying the original call outright is that the sale of the higher level call reduces the amount of money paid out.

A bear spread is the reverse of this process, again using calls. The trader sells the lower striking price and buys the higher; if the bond declines the lower level call price will fall and with it the chances of being called at that level. The purchase at the higher level here provides a modicum of insurance if the strategy goes awry.

Other basic options strategies involve straddles of different varieties. The simplest is the purchase of a put and call at the same striking price. This enables the investor to be flexible if he is uncertain about future market movements. This is similar to a double option in the London over-the-counter option market, offering an investor the same ability in certain common shares. Other varieties involve other combinations of puts and calls in more exotic combinations, but unfortunately go beyond the scope of the present discussion.

The future of fixed interest options in general will depend to a great extent upon the volatility of interest rates in the future; the same sort of volatility that proved such a boon for the futures markets. A particular direction for prices is not as important as the fact that they are volatile, even if it be in one direction only. And they will also have to appeal eventually to the smaller investor for whom the ultimate risks of the futures markets prove too great.

BOND FUTURES OPTIONS

In this survey we have examined instruments which all settle either in cash instruments or in actual cash or deposits. When eurodollar contracts were first introduced, offering the right to receive something other than a security, they were looked upon as quite radical in their own right. Subsequently, options on US Treasury bond futures contracts were conceived of and plans to trade them on the CBT were announced.

This instrument is for all practical purposes almost exactly similar in context and terminology to the bond option described above. But it calls for delivery of a bond futures contract rather than a bond, as does the traditional option. This appears to be taking the concept of futures trading to the last degree. Yet options on futures have a singular allure making them attractive to traders.

The futures option offers the trader the volatility of the futures market plus the limited liability associated with an option. In this respect, it appears that it may be able to pre-empt the option itself by depriving it of its appeal, while retaining the speculative nature of the futures market. It also retains the futures markets' ability to deliver more than one cash instrument against a contract, thereby ensuring that the futures contracts will be extremely price sensitive even in relatively quiet market environments. However, at this stage it is still too early to determine whether these contracts will even succeed, so discussion concerning their individual competitiveness must be postponed for the future.

CONDITIONS FOR SUCCESS IN FUTURES INNOVATION

Many of the contracts introduced into US financial futures markets have proved to be failures. Gold, commercial paper and certificates of deposit failed on the Chicago Board of Trade; short-term Treasury notes, Italian lira, French francs and Dutch guilders failed on the International Monetary Market; most contracts failed on the New York Financial Futures Exchange, with the exception of the stock index. There is no one simple factor that can explain failure in all cases; the roots of failure are manifold. Nor can success or failure be forecast from a simple reading of the early trading volume which a contract scores. Even so, the history of the futures industry is now sufficiently rich to make some tentative propositions about conditions likely to promote the success or failure of new contracts.

First, it is extremely difficult for one futures exchange to launch a contract almost identical to one which already enjoys a liquid market on another exchange. NYFFE and LIFFE have found it impossible to break into the currency futures market, given that an already highly liquid market exists on the IMM. Why should outside traders in foreign exchange choose to put their orders through a new market where there is no assurance of liquidity, when an already liquid market exists elsewhere? Where two successful markets are found in identical contracts (for example, stock index futures on the Chicago Mercantile Exchange and on NYFFE), it will usually be found that they were launched simultaneously. A high probability should not be given to their continued co-survival. At some stage in the future it is likely that for some reason business turnover will rise in one (A) relative to the other (B), and that A will then gain a liquidity advantage. As that occurs, many traders will transfer their business from B to A simply because of liquidity considerations. Thus even if the initial variation in business turnover was due to a short-lived factor, B may never again rise to its feet after that initial factor has ceased to be relevant.

Luck is an important ingredient in the success of futures market innovations, as for most business ventures. Less than a year after the launching of currency futures trading on Chicago's IMM, the US dollar was floated in the foreign exchange markets. This provided the spark that set alight what at first had been a very sluggish activity. The floating of US dollar interest rates in late 1979, when the Federal Reserve switched from targeting interest rates to targeting monetary base growth, provided a powerful boost to interest-rate futures trading. The stock index futures contract on the CME and NYFFE were launched just several weeks before a boom on Wall Street when trading volume reached record highs.

It is an adage of the futures industry that hedgers cannot make a market. The hedger usually takes a position in the market to offset a given risk exposure. He does not trade again until his contract is close to maturity, unlike the active speculator who trades in and out of the market over short intervals of time. If the hedger's underlying risk exposure has terminated as maturity is approached, he does not take out any new futures position. If he still has an underlying risk exposure, he would be likely to enter into a new futures commitment by effecting a spread transaction (dealing for two delivery dates simultaneously). Hedging business that is effected in the spread markets makes a smaller contribution to liquidity of the futures market than does simple outright dealing. The Eurodollar futures contract on the IMM attracted an especially high proportion of hedging relative to speculative interest, illustrated by open interest typically being a high proportion of turnover; but the substantial hedging interest did not prove to be a sufficient condition for the Eurodollar contract to be a success.

Given that speculative trading is important to the success of a contract, it should be designed so as to attract speculative attention. The Eurodollar contract did not have speculative appeal because many participants in US futures markets are not familiar with the Euro-market-place and with how rates are determined there. The gold contract on the Board of Trade proved a failure largely because its size (400 oz) was too great for the small speculator. Speculative traders are concerned to obtain maximum 'play' for a given brokerage fee and margin deposit. Thus, if they are taking a view on the US dollar, the Swiss franc contract is usually more attractive than the Deutsche mark contract, given that the Swiss franc is more sensitive than the mark to changes in the US dollar's international popularity. Indeed, the Swiss franc has been generally a busier contract than the Deutsche mark on the IMM, despite hedging business being considerably more active in the latter. Similarly, if speculators are taking a view on the movement of long-term interest rates, the long-term bond contracts on the CBT offer 'better value for money' (where money is interpreted as brokerage fees and margin) than the short-term (3–4 year) note futures that were listed on the IMM. Indeed, by the early 1980s, the IMM's Treasury note contract had proved a decisive failure.

Futures markets offer to the small trader the possibility of obtaining competitive quotes and often enable him to deal at lower transaction cost than elsewhere. Futures markets thrive on a high volume of retail business; by construction they cannot compete with wholesale markets. It is essential to the success of a futures contract that it can be marketed easily to a large range of retail customers. For example, the stock index futures contract had an immediate appeal to small savers who could, for the first time, deal in a widely diversified portfolio at low transaction costs.

Futures contracts, like other innovations, must be marketed to the general public. The exchange itself usually takes part in the marketing process, by setting up educational programmes and advertising; the exchange's research department must often educate the members about the uses of a new contract so that they can in turn explain it to their clients. Chicago had an easier task in marketing financial futures than the later markets in London and New York, due to its position at the heart of the US agricultural commodity futures business. Broker members of CBT and IMM had among their client lists a large number of corporations already active in the commodity futures markets; it was a small step to interest them in the new financial futures market. Indeed a CBT broker could have his agent on the floor execute orders for his customer both in the grain pits and in Treasury bonds; the floor brokerage function could be shared between the new and old markets. An IMM broker could obtain similar joint economies (on the assumption that he is a member both of the CME and of the IMM) from transacting in both pork bellies and currencies on behalf of clients. Both LIFFE and NYFFE started with the handicap of being insulated from other commodity market floors, so that floor traders lacked the flexibility of their Chicago counterparts.

Complementarity between a new financial futures contract and other contracts traded on the same floor can be an important ingredient in its success. For example, when CD futures were introduced almost simultaneously on the IMM and CBT, traders on the IMM had the comparative advantage that they could lay off positions in the IMM T-bill futures market which was already highly liquid. Scalpers on the IMM were somewhat more competitive than their counterparts on the CBT in quoting for their own inventory during periods when orders for CD futures were bunched in one direction, as they could hedge inventory risk to some extent by taking an opposite position in the T-bill futures market, while waiting for bunching of commercial orders to move in the opposite direction.

A highly liquid spot market existing alongside the futures market has often proved the key to the latter's success. The T-bill futures market has been the most successful of the various interest-rate futures markets, in part because of the depth of the cash market. The existence of a highly liquid cash market allows the complications of variable delivery date and variable name, which beset the CD futures contract, to be avoided and also precludes the danger of a squeeze developing. If there is a significant risk of manipulation in the underlying spot market, many traders would be deterred from participation. Indeed, any suggestion that there has been collusive dealing in the futures market would have a serious negative impact on participation by the public; the gold and silver futures markets suffered a definite setback from the various scandals of the Great Gold Boom in 1979–80.

A liquid spot market alongside the given futures market, usually provides the opportunity for an active cash-futures arbitrage business. Cash-futures arbitrage helps to assure a high level of liquidity in the futures market itself and also provides an opportunity for profitable business by locals on the futures trading floor. In the early stage of a new contract's life, the guarantee of liquidity, which the possibility of cash-futures arbitrage offers, is especially important.

A first step in the launching of a new futures contract is to convince locals on the floor that the new market will offer them significant opportunity for profit. If a scalper is to divert his whole-hearted attention from markets which are already liquid to the new market, he must presumably believe that the market will shortly be successful, and that he will reap substantial compensation for the opportunity cost which he incurs during the run-in when he is gaining experience. On the CBT it has proved difficult to persuade locals to make an effective market in short-term interest-rate futures. Locals there are unwilling to assume spread positions between different delivery months as these cannot be closed by the traditional cash-and-carry operations which are effected in the commodity futures markets or in the T-bond markets; yet spread market dealing is essential to the liquidity of the further off contracts. In the commodity market, if a trader has a long position in say June, matched by a short position in September, he can take delivery in June and hold a covered position of very little risk until re-delivery in September; in the short-term interest-rate futures markets, spreading is more complex (see p. 71).

A futures contract which is not allied to a liquid cash market, and which could not attract a high volume of short-term speculative trading, would probably fail, even were there substantial hedging interest. An example of such a contract would be one based on the CPI-index say 3, 6, 9 and 12 months from the present. The absence of a cash market in the index is in itself a serious handicap to liquidity. Furthermore, the index is itself subject to revision and published in arrears; cash settlement as in the stock futures or Eurodollar futures market could not be applied easily. In normal circumstances, inflation expectations do not change from day to day, and the level of speculative trading would be likely to be very low.

Forecasting the growth of the futures industry is an especially hazardous activity. Experience has shown that periods of sharp growth have been related to developments that were not predicted by the market innovators themselves. Certainly the futures industry is not a low-risk sector of the economy. Many contracts fail, and whole markets set up at large cost can prove to be expensive write-offs for their founding members. Yet the financial futures industry has reached an old enough age to have a history, and this can now be used increasingly as a laboratory against which to test new ideas for innovation.

NOTE

1. In options markets, the term 'premium' is used in a different context than in the money and bond markets. Premium means the entire price paid for an option. It does not refer to the difference between nominal and market value. Hence, out-of-the-money options have premiums as do in-the-money options.

Glossary

arbitrage   the process of buying and selling securities simultaneously in different markets to take advantage of price differentials

backwardation   a state of price deterioration where the next offered price is lower than the previous bid on the same instrument

basis   the difference in price (or yield) between a cash market instrument and its futures counterpart

bid   the quoted price at which a security or future may be sold

call   an option to buy, at a specific price, for a specific period of time

covering   the act of buying a financial instrument in order to deliver against a short sale

CD   certificate delivery, one of the two methods of delivery for GNMA futures contracts; this method calls for actual delivery of GNMA certificates themselves, determined by a yield-maintenance formula

CD   a certificate of deposit, issued by banks in both the domestic and euromarkets; unlike a normal term deposit it is a liquid instrument supported by an active secondary market

CDR   collateralised depository receipt, the second of the two methods used in delivering against a GNMA contract; this method calls for delivery of a receipt backed by actual securities themselves and is determined by a principal-maintenance formula

CFTC   the Commodity Futures Trading Commission, empowered by an act of Congress in 1974 with the duty to regulate all commodity futures trading in the USA

171

cheapness a term used to describe the least expensive cash security that can be delivered against a short futures position

contango an expected state of security price rise when investors sometimes leverage themselves to buy

coupon the amount of stated interest paid on a bond, GNMA, or certificate of deposit

CPI consumer price index, a composite index of goods purchased by individuals intended to measure the rate of inflation

delivery month the specific month in which a futures contract closes

discount the amount below par (100) at which a low coupon bond or ordinary Treasury bill is quoted; it is normally stated in full percentage points and fractions thereof

fill or kill an order placed with a futures broker meaning that it must be executed in its entirety at the stipulated place or immediately discarded

forward the price of a contract in the traditional foreign exchange market, dated for delivery in the near future

GTC good till cancelled order; placed with a broker by an investor who signifies a specific price for his order with no specific period of time in mind

LIBOR the London Interbank Offered Rate for euro-dollars; sometimes also used to describe sterling

limit an order placed with a broker setting strict price restrictions upon execution

locals those speculators and market makers drawn from the indigenous population who make up the trading backbone of floorbrokers on a futures exchange

long hedge a strategy whereby one purchases futures for intended delivery in order to lock in today's interest rates

margin the amount of money actually needed to open a futures position

nearby the price of a future in the delivery month closest to the spot month

offer the quoted price at which a security or future may be purchased

open interest the amount of contracts outstanding on any type of futures contract or listed option

par cap a stipulation found in the GNMA certificate delivery contract stating that no cash securities priced above par can be delivered against a short position

partly paid a method used in the British gilt market and in the eurobond market where a new issue is initially offered at a fraction of par, the balance being due on a specific date

premium the amount above par (100) that a high coupon bond or high-yielding Treasury bill is quoted; it is normally stated in full percentage points and fractions thereof

principal maintenance a method of determining how many cash Treasury bonds, gilts or GNMAs are to be delivered against a futures contract; it uses a factor to determine the amount of securities to be delivered, based upon the notional yield of the futures contract

price limit the amount of market price movement allowed a particular futures contract in any one trading day

put an option to sell, at a specific price, for a specific period of time

roll-over a technique whereby a futures position is closed out and immediately extended by opening another farther into the future

scalpers those floorbrokers on an exchange whose major function is to take advantage of minor price discrepancies

short hedge a strategy whereby one sells (short) futures in order to profit from ensuing interest-rate rises

spot month the closest delivery month on a particular futures contract

spot price the price of the spot month on a particular futures contract

spread the differential between the bid and ask quotes on a cash or futures price

stagging a British term referring to the purchase and quick sale of a security without the intention of paying for it in full

straddle a trading strategy involving both long and short positions on the same futures contract or option; usually done at a similar price in the same delivery month

yield maintenance a method of determining how many bonds are to be delivered against a futures position; in antithesis to the principal-maintenance contract, it uses price of a bond as the crucial factor in calculating delivery amount rather than principal equivalent.

Index

175